MW01073393

"This powerful and insight
manifest in mortal and fal
faith and radical love! Ben.__ ,
and compassion more than ever in this Trump moment!"

—CORNEL WEST, philosopher, political activist,
and author of *Democracy Matters*

"This is the book you have been waiting for, whether you know it or
not. In our troubled times (which times aren't?) we are led to wonder
if scripture can say anything that really matters. But in those parts of
the Bible we often read the least, OT scholar Jason Bembry has found a
treasure trove of riches that address our most vexing questions . . . But
perhaps more important than the particular issues he addresses, he
teaches us what a truly Biblical STANCE in our world might look like."

—RANDY HARRIS, Abilene Christian University

"Professor Jason Bembry is a gifted scholar of the Bible and Biblical languages, and he also firmly believes that the trenchant voices of
the Bible's prophets remain deeply relevant for our fractured modern
world. Thus, Bembry describes the bravery of the Bible's prophets
and then seamlessly weaves into his discussion courageous modern
prophetic figures such as Rosa Parks, Myles Horton, Dorothy Day,
Martin Luther King, Jr., Delores Huerta, and Cesar Chavez. This is a
priceless volume."

—CHRISTOPHER ROLLSTON, George Washington University

"Bembry skillfully brings into conversation the Old Testament prophets and modern-day truth-tellers in ways that are mutually enriching,
freeing these ancient voices from domestication while at the same
time offering those who would dare speak truth to power in our day
timely lessons from this oft-ignored Biblical tradition. An inspiring
and challenging call to all who desire in our day to walk more faith-
fully in the way of justice and truth."

—PHILIP D. KENNESON, Milligan College

"If you've ever wanted to live in the spirit of the Hebrew prophets, heeding the call to 'enact justice and the love of mercy and to walk with your God humbly' (Mic 6:8), this book is a must. Be prepared to be challenged and emboldened by rarely told stories of the biblical prophets and their contemporary exemplars. Bembry unlocks the power of the prophetic tradition in a moment when the church so desperately needs it."

—MIRIAM Y. PERKINS, Emmanuel Christian Seminary at Milligan

Walking in the Prophetic Tradition

Walking in the Prophetic Tradition

*Models of Speaking Truth
and Acting in Love for Everyday People*

Jason A. Bembry

Foreword by Miriam Perkins

CASCADE *Books* • Eugene, Oregon

WALKING IN THE PROPHETIC TRADITION
Models of Speaking Truth and Acting in Love for Everyday People

Cascade Books
An Imprint of Wipf and Stock Publishers
199 W. 8th Ave., Suite 3
Eugene, OR 97401

www.wipfandstock.com

PAPERBACK ISBN: 978-1-5326-4980-6
HARDCOVER ISBN: 978-1-5326-4981-3
EBOOK ISBN: 978-1-5326-4982-0

Cataloguing-in-Publication data:

Names: Bembry, Jason A., author. | Perkins, Miriam, foreword.

Title: Walking in the prophetic tradition : models of speaking truth and acting in love for everyday people / Jason A. Bembry ; foreword by Miriam Perkins.

Description: Eugene, OR: Cascade Books, 2016. | Includes bibliographical references and index.

Identifiers: ISBN 978-1-5326-4980-6 (paperback). | ISBN 978-1-5326-4981-3 (hardcover). | ISBN 978-1-5326-4982-0 (ebook).

Subjects: LCSH: Prophets. | Bible—Prophets—Criticism, interpretation, etc. | Social justice—Religious aspects. | Day, Dorothy, 1897–1980. | Horton, Myles, 1905–1990. |Chavez, Cesar, 1927–1993. | King, Martin Luther, Jr., 1929–1968. | Campbell, Will D., 1924–2013.| West, Cornel.

Classification: BR1700.2 B37 2018 (print). | BR1700.2 (ebook).

Manufactured in the U.S.A.   OCTOBER 26, 2018

A portion of chapter three appeared in my article "Cornel West, Biblical Transparency, and American Historical Amnesia," *Theology Today* 68(2) July 2011, published by Sage Publishing. Used here by permission.

This book is lovingly dedicated to my parents, Wallace and Anne Bembry, who taught me to love the Bible and the prophetic tradition from a very young age. Their love and commitment to me throughout my life is incalculable and their lives have always constituted a model for love and justice. I hope this book can symbolize for them a small token of my deep gratitude.

Contents

Foreword

Are you a reader who suspects you have never been adequately introduced to the prophets in any substantive way? If so, read on. Many readers may be familiar with the summary statement of Micah 6:8: to love mercy, and do justice, and walk humbly with God. Others may readily bring to mind the beautiful readings from the prophets that surround the Advent season (Isaiah 40; Micah 5). Yet this book is for readers dissatisfied with such brief sketches. *Walking in the Prophetic Tradition* invites an encounter with the broader vision and vocation of the Hebrew prophets.

This book is also for readers troubled by the seemingly intractable injustices of our world: poverty, racism, sexual violence, addiction, immigration, migration, migrant labor, and systemic human displacements of all kinds. This book is for those readers even more troubled when Christians appear indifferent or silent about these injustices, which are well-worn in some neighborhoods and communities and ever more visible in others. *Walking in the Prophetic Tradition* invites reflection on the startling contemporary relevance and applicability of the Hebrew prophets.

Walking in the Prophetic Tradition helpfully points the reader toward the prophetic spirit of visionary people of faith in recent United States history. Dorothy Day and Martin Luther King, Jr., mentioned by Pope Francis in his 2015 address to Congress as Americans who have called him to more radical faith, are the subject of this book. Dr. Jason Bembry expands the horizon by additionally including the remarkable work of César Chávez, Myles

Horton, Cornel West, and Will Campbell. Understanding the legacy of these saint-like activists—an African American philosopher, an African American minister and civil rights leader, a Latino labor activist, a woman lay Catholic, an Appalachian educator, and a southern Caucasian Baptist minister—has a great deal to do with the boldness of the Hebrew prophetic tradition and the diversity of its contemporary expressions.

Yet a few fair words of warning.

Christian readers may wish this book was more explicitly about Jesus. In those moments, bear in mind the canonical importance of the Hebrew prophets in their own right. While the subject of this book is not Jesus, it is impossible to grasp his self-understanding, his challenging teachings, his ministry among outcasts, his liberating and determined faithfulness to God, apart from his prophetic forbearers. His "good news for the oppressed" was a prophetic ministry (Luke 4:18–19; Isaiah 61). Readers of other religious traditions will appreciate where this prophetic impulse resonates with their own tradition's forbearers of prophetic witness.

Walking in the Prophetic Tradition breaks through the social and religious inertia that keeps readers alienated from both biblical and contemporary prophetic voices. This book will likely make engaged readers uncomfortable. The reasons are not easy to outline succinctly. But they include the color of your skin, and the racial diversity, or lack thereof, of your churches and schools and cities. The reasons include your level of affluence and presumptions around where your resources and gifts belong. They include a disquieting and alarming desire for a faith that makes no real demands of you, nor builds any bonds of tangible human consolation. This book can serve to remind communities how to honor and live into the prophetic spirit day by day. As Dr. Bembry so trenchantly outlines, the prophets call us to new and renewed practices of: humility, speaking truth to power, honesty about our nation's complicated history, integrity in worship, advocacy among the poor, concern for workers, and a commitment to justice.

Nonetheless, you are in good hands. Not many scholars risk their guarded academic status by writing in an accessible voice and with Christian communities in mind. I am privileged to work daily with several such scholars, and Dr. Jason Bembry is among the best. As his colleague for nearly a decade, I well recognize that this book is not only evidence of his deep knowledge of the Hebrew Bible. It is also a testimony to how years of reading the prophets shapes the substance of his moral commitments, unveils for him a more honest accounting of racism's legacy, emboldens his advocacy for justice, and informs the occasionally hard word I have seen him land in a room. Above all else, this book speaks to his sometimes understated, but no less fierce, love for the God whose voice thunders through the prophets.

The prophets can have a refining and emboldening effect on a human life. So read with care and an open heart. Share this book with kindred spirits in your communities. And pass it along to any who long with you for a more just world.

Miriam Perkins
Emmanuel Christian Seminary at Milligan
September 2018

Acknowledgments

This project is the culmination of a long journey. Its genesis extends to my doctoral program where my eyes were first opened by Cornel West in 2000. His eloquence and passion about the importance of the Old Testament prophetic tradition set me on the path to see the deeper implications of all the work I was doing in the department of Near Eastern Languages and Civilizations at that time. Even back to my undergraduate days Randy Harris, my first theology professor and the person most responsible for inspiring me toward education as a career, pointed me toward West and suggested I read everything he wrote.

The final shape of this book is the result of teaching a class on the prophets at Milligan College and Emmanuel Christian Seminary for more than a decade. I am deeply indebted to the students who engaged this class and worked through the material to provide an enriching dialogue about the words of the Old Testament prophets in the ancient world and the implications of that work for today. A number of those classes read parts of early drafts of this project as assignments for the course, and I appreciate their feedback.

A number of colleagues have served as conversation partners and sounding boards for the ideas in this book—Kip Elolia, Miriam Perkins, and Adam Bean, my colleagues at Emmanuel. A special thanks is extended to Miriam Perkins for providing tremendous insight on a number of points in the book and graciously agreeing to write the foreword. I also want to recognize my dear friend and colleague Christopher Rollston at George Washington

University, who graciously mentored me and befriended me when I first came to Emmanuel. Our friendship is a true gift, strengthened during hard times. Hardly a week goes by without my passing his old office just down from mine and fondly remembering a time when our conversations were just a few steps away.

Nathaniel Greene was one of the first students I had during the earliest formation of this material, and he has been a constant source of encouragement in the quest to bring this book to publication. I also want to thank Phil Kenneson, my colleague at Milligan College, who was willing to read an early draft and make numerous helpful suggestions about the direction of the project.

A very special thanks goes to another dear friend, colleague, and fellow NELC-y, Gene McGarry, whose editorial genius and tremendous insight continues to amaze me, and whose friendship I deeply cherish. I am also grateful for the encouragement from another NELC-y, Jonathan Kline, whom I met through conversation about this book project.

I have also had a number of very skillful teaching assistants at Emmanuel who have served as proofreaders and interlocutors for the text and the ideas in this book. I mention them here with gratitude—Jack Weinbender, Serena McMillan, Patrick Harvey, Renata Vicente, Kelli Allen, and Kolby Pinkston.

Finally, I could do nothing without acknowledging my wife, Fay Hardison Bembry, whose love and support has sustained me for over twenty-five years. Fay has believed in me and my work even when I did not. Her love is an ever-flowing stream.

Introduction

PROPHECY IS ONE OF the most frequently misunderstood concepts in the Bible. Questions abound concerning what prophecy meant in ancient Israel and what it might mean for people of faith today. Too often biblical prophecy is assumed to refer to predictions of future events, in keeping with the way English speakers normally employ the verb "to prophesy." This book addresses a different aspect of biblical prophecy, one that has little to do with predicting the future. The kind of prophecy this book examines is found in the teachings of many Old Testament prophets, people who took great risks to deliver the often difficult divine message to the those around them. They spoke the uncomfortable word, the admonition and correction directed at improper behavior.

Prophecy, as it is described in this book, is a call that urges people—all people—to right living. The message of the biblical prophets is often addressed to those in power but it does not apply only to them. These prophets speak out of humility before God. They offer direction in the form of calls to proper conduct undergirded by lives of integrity that bear witness to God's work. The biblical prophets were spokespersons for God, messengers who spoke truth to power. They reminded the people of their checkered past—the times when they did not follow God's ways. The prophets indicted those who were hypocritical in worship; they called for protection of poor people and immigrants and for proper treatment of working people. These messengers called for justice—right living—and they took courageous risks to bring the divine word to the people. These are the themes of this book, and these themes are the aspects of prophecy that everyday people can enact.

Engaging the biblical prophets requires that we read the biblical testimony about their lives, and that we do so carefully since our definition of prophecy can be skewed by notions of prediction. Since the world of the Bible and the world of the twenty-first century are clearly different, readers and interpreters of the prophetic stories in the Bible must carefully examine the texts to ensure a proper understanding of what God was doing in the lives of those prophets and how the lessons of the prophetic teachings can be embraced by people today. This book aims to do just that, by approaching the prophets as ambassadors of divine instruction on how to live. This book seeks to discover the message of the biblical prophets and to draw attention to modern people who have emulated them.

WALKING AS A METAPHOR FOR LIFE

The title of this book employs the metaphor of walking as a way to describe the course of one's life. It is a metaphor deeply rooted in the traditions of the Hebrew Bible and carries forward into the New Testament. In the Hebrew Bible, "walking in the ways of God" is synonymous with living properly. Because the metaphor is so important for the idea behind this book, I want to take a moment to demonstrate just how thoroughly pervasive this biblical idiom is. The injunction to "walk in my/his [Yahweh's] ways" is found often in Deuteronomy (5:33; 8:6; 10:12; 11:22; 30:16).[1] To walk in the ways of a human being, on the other hand, can indicate either proper or improper behavior. This figurative use of walking appears often in the books of 1–2 Kings where a king is either praised or condemned depending on the ways in which he "walked." Kings who walked in the ways of Jeroboam son of Nebat (1 Kgs 16:2, 19, 26, 31), on the one hand, were deemed bad. Yet those who walked

---

1. All Bible translations are my own.

in the ways of David (1 Kgs 3:3; 9:4; 2 Kgs 22:2) were considered righteous. Further examples of the metaphor of walking can be seen in the prophets (Ezek 11:20; 20:19; 36:27; Zech 3:7; Micah 6:8), the Psalms (26:11; 89:30; 143:8), and Proverbs (2:20; 15:21). In the New Testament, the appropriation of walking as a metaphor for living can be found in Eph 2:10, Rom 13:13, 2 Cor 5:7, and Col 2:6.

I use this metaphor in the title to honor the biblical tradition, on the one hand, but also to illustrate how heeding the message of the prophets is much like a journey on a path. At times walking can be difficult and sometimes the path is not always clear or easy. Fatigue and uncertainty can thwart progress and jeopardize completion of the trip. Journeying on a path can be a communal act as well, as travelers seek guidance and receive encouragement on the way, and also confront obstacles and overcome difficulty together. In this metaphorical landscape the biblical prophets serve as guides, assisting travelers on their way, warning of obstacles and blind alleys, and witnessing to the proper approach a traveler should take along the path. I also invoke the voices of twentieth- and twenty-first-century people in this book to illustrate modern lives that have traveled this path. I hope that these figures, like the biblical prophets, can become fellow travelers on this path, aiding all who seek to understand and live out the ways of God's people. This book is my attempt to guide and encourage us all along that way, and to help recognize and overcome obstacles on the path of a life lived within the prophetic tradition.

WHAT DOES IT MEAN TO PROPHESY?

Walking or living our lives within the prophetic tradition presumes that we all understand what prophesying means in the biblical tradition. Yet, as I indicated earlier, prophecy is often vaguely understood or clearly misunderstood by many well-meaning Christians, and this has been true for a long time. Prophets are referred to by a number of titles in Hebrew. The word for prophet, *nabi'*, simply means "one who is summoned," a term well suited for God's spokespersons. The feminine form of this word, rendered "prophetess," is applied to five women in the Old Testament (Exod 15:20; Judg 4:4; 2 Kgs 22:14; 2 Chron 34:22; Isa 8:3; Neh 6:14). Prophets are also given the title "seer," the literal meaning of the Hebrew words *ro'eh* and *ḥozeh*, and these terms are probably rooted in the notion that God's spokespersons saw visions. The phrase "man of God" is also used of some of the biblical prophets. The biblical terminology itself, however, provides only limited information about the act of prophesying.

When we move beyond the lexicon of prophecy and turn to the phenomenon of prophetic activity in the Bible, we enter a realm that has fascinated many for millennia. There are many helpful books and articles that outline all the ways that prophets functioned in ancient Israel and Judah and in the surrounding ancient Near East.[2] In this book our examination of prophetic work will be more focused on themes shared among the prophets, a topic I will address in greater detail later in this introduction. At this point let us simply note an important obstacle to a proper understanding of the ancient practice of prophecy, an obstacle that can cloud our inquiry. Take, for example, what I noted earlier about the use in English of the verb "to prophesy." To most native English speakers, to prophesy is simply to predict the future. This meaning is certainly present in the Bible, and it is especially important for Christians, who often assert that biblical prophecy, particularly prophecy found in the Old Testament, points to the future in general and foretells aspects of the ministry of Jesus in particular. Yet when we take a closer look at the Old Testament prophets, we see that predicting the future is actually a small part of what they do. In fact, Old Testament prophets have more to say about their past and their present than they do about events centuries later. Even so, the primary understanding of prophecy as prediction is an approach that has a long history. During the first few centuries of the Christian tradition, interpreters of the Bible had a marked penchant for pressing Old Testament prophetic texts into service

2. See, for example, Blenkinsopp, *History of Prophecy*. For the broader phenomena in the cultural backdrop of biblical Israel, see Nissinen, *Prophecy*.

as pointers to Jesus.[3] Those particular texts became central to the Christian appropriation of Old Testament prophecy, fueling the notion that the prophets were primarily predictors whose words anticipated Jesus.

Consider the following examples. Ambrose (337–397 CE), bishop of Milan, told Augustine (354–430 CE), his student, to read Isaiah because "he is more plainly a foreteller of the gospel and of the calling of the gentiles than are the others."[4] Indeed, Jerome (347–420 CE) wrote that "Isaiah should be considered more of an evangelist than a prophet because he describes all the mysteries of Christ and the church so clearly that you would think he is composing a history of what has already happened rather than prophesying about what is to come."[5] An unintended effect of this interpretive move in the Christian tradition is that it has diminished the impact of the prophetic voices that addressed the past and the present within modern Christian circles. Prophets spoke truth to power structures, unmasked hypocrisy, reminded their fellow Israelites of their past, advocated for the marginalized, and called for justice for all people. This commitment often meant that what the prophets had to say was not always welcomed by those who benefited from those power structures and the status quo. As Abraham J. Heschel notes, the prophet is a human iconoclast who "employs notes one octave too high for our ears," signaling the difficulty many have with the prophetic word, whether it be too painful to hear or too difficult to implement.[6] This book seeks to uncover that particular iconoclastic aspect of biblical prophecy, an aspect that is central to the Old Testament prophetic tradition.

When prophets spoke critically of the authorities in ancient times, efforts were often made to silence them. Kings would

---

3. Skarsaune, "Development of Scriptural Interpretation," 376; and Miller, *Helping Jesus Fulfill Prophecy*, 19.

4. Sawyer, *Fifth Gospel*, 2.

5. Sawyer, *Fifth Gospel*, 2. Sawyer notes that the same sentiment is seen in Isidore of Seville (560–636) and centuries later in Hugh of Saint Cher (ca. 1200–1263).

6. Heschel, *Prophets*, 12.

imprison these prophets or kill them, courtiers would try to minimize their influence, and false prophets would attempt to suppress them in order to secure their own exclusive access to the circles of power. Speaking a word of prophecy in the biblical period was dangerous at times and often constituted an act requiring profound courage—courage to cut across the grain of society, and courage to risk life and limb to carry the divine message to the king, to other leaders, and to the people.

This book is an attempt to recover that kind of courage as an inspiration for "everyday people"—people who might not have direct access to significant economic or political power and influence but who can nevertheless speak up and make a difference in our world at this time. I hope that what is in these pages will inspire people to action. I fully admit that I possess a conviction that everyday people can make a positive difference in the world. I do believe that all can engage in the kind of things the biblical prophets stood for. This perspective is one reason I want to offer these pages to anyone regardless of position, status, or level of education. It is my conviction that this book can help all obtain a better grasp of this courageous, truth-telling sensibility exhibited by the Old Testament prophets. By becoming familiar with this perspective, all who follow God can be equipped to recognize modern people who exemplify the same passion and courage manifested by the prophets, and who can also inspire others to join in that tradition of standing for what is right and just.

Yet another reason I want to speak to everyday people is because of the broader freedom that people whose livelihood does not depend on interpreting the Bible may have in carrying forth the prophetic word from the biblical tradition. Let me be clear about what I mean here. Often it is the case that those who are employed to teach the Bible have a difficult time speaking truth to power in the manner of the prophetic tradition. The people I am talking about are preachers, ministers, rabbis, bishops, teachers, and professors—people who are employed by churches, synagogues, religiously affiliated schools, colleges, universities, publishing houses, and more. These are people who often know just what the biblical prophets are about. They know that the prophets speak the uncomfortable truth to power structures. Yet they often hesitate to teach and exercise this particular aspect of the prophets' work for fear of being treated like those prophets. The end result is that the prophetic message is often never heard, in many circles, from the ones best equipped to teach it.

I do not mean to imply that people who are not employed by religiously affiliated entities have an easier time speaking the truth to power. They do not. Virtually no one can walk in the prophetic tradition, stand for what is right, and speak the truth to power without courting some potential ill effect. We all must have courage to walk the path I describe in this book. Everyday people who work for fairness, truth, and justice have a lot to lose, no less than Bible teachers, ministers, and religious leaders. Yet by virtue of sheer numbers, those who make their living apart from religious or faith-based institutions can bring the prophetic voice into virtually all walks of life through friends, coworkers, colleagues, and family connections.

So it is my hope that all people—those who earn their livelihood from religious institutions and those who do not—will have the courage to walk in the prophetic tradition and muster the fortitude to stand for what is right and to speak the truth in love to the power structures all around us in the workplace, the community, and the local church, all the way up to the highest levels of power in our world.

I write as a Christian and in what follows it will become clear that I speak primarily to the issues and concerns that Christians will find familiar. Yet the prophetic tradition in the Hebrew Bible can bridge the divide between Judaism, Islam, and Christianity, the major faith traditions informed by the words of these spokespersons for God. I hope there is much in this book that can assist all people of all faiths. The themes around which this book is centered can speak instructively to all communities and can perhaps remind people of faith that what unites us is greater than that which divides us.

THE OBSTACLE OF THE CONSTANTINIAN SHIFT

The tradition of speaking the hard truth to people who need to hear it has always been fraught with difficulties. The ancient prophets we read about in the Bible had a challenging mission, and those who try to emulate them can expect some level of resistance. This seems to be a persistent pattern of human behavior throughout history. Jesus himself reminded his disciples of this aspect of the prophetic tradition when he said to them, "Blessed are you when people insult you and persecute you and falsely say all kinds of evil against you because of me. Rejoice and be glad for your reward in heaven is great. For in the same way they persecuted the prophets who were before you" (Matt 5:11–12). So it is important to recognize the perennial nature of the difficulty of this tradition's path. It is also important for Christians to recognize a particular hurdle within our own tradition that made this prophetic enterprise especially challenging, a hurdle that continues to bedevil most Christians everywhere but particularly those whose history places them in the so-called "western Christian tradition" that developed out of the Greco-Roman world of antiquity. This hurdle is known as the "Constantinian Shift," a phrase that refers to the profound transformation that early Christianity underwent around the time of the Roman Emperor Constantine (306–337 CE). During this shift, the church was transformed from a persecuted or barely tolerated faith community whose members were mainly marginalized peoples into an accepted and eventually mainstream religion. This shift in the status of Christian believers from marginal to central had a profound effect on the way Christians would come to view themselves, their traditions, and their relationship with the power of the state.

According to tradition Constantine had a vision before an important battle at the Tiber River in 312 CE where he faced the army of his rival Maxentius, a fellow Roman who laid claim to the western Roman Empire. Before the battle a heavenly voice spoke to Constantine saying, "Conquer by this," and he saw an image formed by combining the Greek letters *chi* and *rho*, the first two letters of "Christ." The emperor purportedly ordered his army to carry this symbol into battle by emblazoning these two letters on their shields, supposing that this gesture would ensure their success at the Battle of Milvian Bridge. Tradition maintains that this military victory led Constantine to issue the Edict of Milan, which removed Christianity from the list of illegal religions. Although much has been made of the Battle of Milvian Bridge as a turning point in the status of Christians in Roman society, it is important to note that Constantine had already showed a willingness to promote religious tolerance in the empire. In 311 CE the emperor issued the Edict of Toleration, which permitted the practice of different religions in his realm.[7] Even so, the transformation that took place in those few years was rather substantial. Christian communities that had seen earlier generations persecuted and in some cases martyred for their faith now found themselves embraced by the surrounding culture. This transformation not only seduced Christians into a cozy relationship with the ruling powers of the day, it also domesticated the Christian message, making it easier to translate into the cultural language of Imperial Rome. The early Christian rhetoric that constituted an indictment of power in the name of Jesus the Christ, the son of God slain by the ruling powers of the world, was softened so as not to offend.

This transformation extended to the way the Old Testament prophets were read and appropriated too. Even before Constantine, early Christian interpreters mostly approached the Old Testament with the intention of making all of its contents point to Jesus as the fulfillment of God's work in the world. One need only read the Gospel of Matthew to see how this interpretive enterprise was operative at an elementary stage of the early Christian experience. Two examples will be sufficient to illustrate this point. First, in Matt 1:23 the prophet Isaiah is cited as a witness to the virgin birth of Jesus. Matthew cites the book of Isaiah (7:14): "Behold, a virgin shall conceive and bear a son and his name shall be called Emmanuel." In the same vein Matt 2:15 provides a prophetic

7. For more on these important years in Constantine's rule, see Reimer, *Christians and War*, 68–71.

anticipation of the episode when Joseph and Mary flee to Egypt with the baby Jesus to escape the wrath of Herod. Here the gospel writer cites Hosea 11:1 as a predictive prophetic pointer to this event. In both cases Matthew prefaces the quote from the prophets with the assertion, "This was to fulfill what the Lord had spoken by the prophet," clearly demonstrating the predictive interpretive enterprise.

Reading the prophets as predictors of Jesus also helped nascent Christianity appropriate the Hebrew Bible in a way that helped to distinguish the new religion from the Judaism of the day. While many early Christians were Jews, with the passage of time the divide between the two faith communities grew larger. By showing how the prophets of the Hebrew Bible (and the Greek translation of the Hebrew Bible, the Septuagint) pointed to Jesus in so many ways, Christian interpreters could claim that their reading of what later came to be called the Old Testament was superior to that of their Jewish counterparts. Thus, there was a polemic value to the interpretive lens that Christians applied to the prophets that cannot be discounted.

In the first centuries of the Common Era, the will to enlist the prophets as witnesses to Jesus overshadowed the prophetic words that questioned the powers that be and spoke a word of correction. When the Constantinian Shift provided a further motive to downplay those words of critique, the domestication of the prophets achieved a new level of success. In light of the sermons and writings that have survived from the fourth century onward, it is rare to find biblical interpreters active in those days who point to the prophets as models for confronting power structures.[8]

Of course, the factors that motivated early interpreters are numerous and complex. Yet it is clear that these two impulses— the desire to reconcile Christianity and the state, and the urge to apply what one might call the "Christo-predictive" interpretive

---

8. The tension between confrontation of power and accommodation thereof can be seen in the New Testament: the apocalyptic voice of Revelation speaks of the prostitute of Babylon as a cipher for Rome (Rev 17:3–10), while Paul's letter to the Roman Christians enjoins them to be subject to the governing authorities (Rom 13:1).

lens to the Hebrew Bible—had a profound impact on the way Old Testament prophets were understood among many Christians. Unfortunately, both impulses continue to have a strong impact on Christians today. The result of this interpretive reality is that the prophets continue to be domesticated: they are read in such a way that their indictment of power remains unrealized in many contemporary Christian circles.

In this book I hope to call Christians to rethink these two influential impulses and to return to the biblical prophets with a renewed willingness to let them speak out today, liberated from the domesticating strictures that have often been placed upon them. I hope we can hear them speak in all their undomesticated, untamed wildness, allowing them to pierce our very souls so that we can see ourselves and the world around us as we should.

THE STRUCTURE OF THIS BOOK

In the chapters that follow I examine a number of Old Testament prophets who provide us with ancient models for the kind of humility and courage required to speak the truth to the powers of our day. Not every prophet who appears in the Hebrew Bible is discussed in this book. Biblical prophets vary widely in many ways, including the level to which they exhibit the courage to speak a confrontational word to the powers of their day. What follows is a selection of biblical prophets whom I consider to be touchstones of the tradition of courageous willingness to confront the powers of the world with a call to right living. Some will be well known to readers of the Bible, while others may seem obscure. Some of these prophets appear in many biblical stories while some are known from only a single episode. All exhibit courage and a willingness to tell the truth as they speak a word from God to those who need to hear it. These prophets constitute a lineage of sorts, a tradition, some might say a "witness" to the way God has worked in the world, speaking the divine word through the mouths of men and women of the past who risked much to carry out their mission.

Although this book is not an exhaustive examination of the ancient context of these prophets historically and textually, I provide relevant information about the background of individual books so that we can appreciate the kinds of pressures the prophets themselves faced as they spoke their words. Additionally this book couples these ancient voices with the voices of modern figures in the United States. These modern lives will help to construct a clearer picture of what it might look like to walk in the prophetic tradition today. To be sure, connecting ancient sensibilities with modern ones is a bit of a subjective enterprise. By bringing these voices to the discussion of the modern day application of biblical prophecy, I am by no means trying to argue that these moderns are actual prophets. None of the modern people I present in this book ever claimed to be a prophet, nor am I trying to suggest that they are perfect or have some kind of special divinely appointed status. Rather, it seems to me that these individuals have been careful students of the Old Testament prophetic tradition and exemplify that fact in the lives that they lived. I want to point to certain aspects of their lives as a kind of reflective tool or lens that might give us a glimpse of how we can embody the same kind of commitment to standing for what is right and just and speaking the truth in love.

I have chosen to explore in detail eight prophetic themes: prophetic humility, speaking truth to power, historic sensibility, indictment of empty religiosity, concern for the poor, attention to the needs of working people, the importance of justice, and courageous risk. Each of these themes is addressed by more than one prophet, which demonstrates the emphasis that is placed on these eight subjects in the biblical witness. The themes illustrate concerns that transcended the single ministry of any one prophetic representative. The recurrence of these concerns in more than one prophetic voice not only indicates their importance in the biblical tradition, but it also suggests that they represent pervasive and enduring problems that confront every generation. The eight themes thus constitute the basis for our examination of modern voices that exhibit the same concerns. The modern examples I use in this book are Dorothy Day, César Chávez, Martin L. King Jr., Myles

Horton, Will Campbell, and Cornel West. Isaiah's words of humility and Moses' and Jeremiah's words of unworthiness are translated into a modern setting through the lives of Will Campbell, César Chávez, and Dorothy Day. Hosea's and Jeremiah's honest assessment of Israel's past is illustrated by Cornel West. Will Campbell and César Chávez take up Isaiah's and Amos's criticism of empty religious ritual. Dorothy Day, César Chávez, Myles Horton, and Will Campbell share the concern Amos, Ezekiel, and Jeremiah had for marginalized people—outsiders and immigrants as well as impoverished people who are unable to support themselves, and what today would be called the "working poor." We will turn to Martin Luther King Jr. as an embodiment of the passion for justice or proper conduct exhibited by Isaiah, Jeremiah, Ezekiel, and Hosea. All of the modern voices we hear in this book demonstrate the prophetic courage necessary to take the risk of speaking the truth to power, as did all the biblical prophets we will encounter in this book. It is my hope that by considering a few of these contemporary parallels, we might become better equipped to recognize these prophetic features in others around us, and perhaps cultivate these features within ourselves.

1

Prophetic Humility as a Starting Point

To BEGIN THE JOURNEY of walking in the prophetic tradition, a stance of humility is absolutely essential. No one appreciates an arrogant gadfly who strolls around criticizing everyone about everything, never cognizant of the way in which his or her critique applies to himself or herself. Sinclair Lewis created a literary character that came to symbolize such sentiment in the twentieth-century American context. The name of the title character of Lewis's novel *Elmer Gantry* became synonymous with religious hypocrisy. The book was a best seller in 1927 and set Lewis on track to win the Nobel Prize in Literature a few years later. Elmer Gantry was a seminary dropout who went on to become a traveling Christian evangelist preaching piety and chastity all while carousing and embracing one-night stands with women wherever he traveled. Lewis's character became the archetypal hypocritic churchman amidst the cultural clashes involving fundamentalist Christians and the prevailing cultural ideas and practices. In 1960 the character was brought to life on the screen by Burt Lancaster in a performance that won him an Academy Award for Best Actor. The film's popularity renewed the role of Elmer Gantry and his hypocritical piety as a cultural icon among audiences throughout the US. The flawed preacher serves as a cautionary tale for all who speak a word of correction without the requisite integrity and the commitment to live in conformity with that message.

In order to walk in the prophetic tradition one must have a deep appreciation for human imperfection. For it is only when one has a deep sense of one's own failings and one's own inability to walk in this path perfectly, that one is able to speak with any kind of authority in people's lives. Several of the biblical prophets demonstrate this kind of self-knowledge when they are about to begin their prophetic ministries. The "call narratives"—stories that recount how the individual prophets began their work—can provide a clear glimpse of the humility with which these prophets approached their tasks. In this first chapter, three prophets, Moses, Jeremiah, and Isaiah, will illustrate the kind of foundation that is essential for walking in the ways of the biblical prophets.

Unfortunately, only a few prophetic call narratives have been preserved. How Nathan, Elijah, Micah, the prophetess Huldah, and many others started their work of prophecy is simply not recounted in the Bible. The narratives that are included, however, express a theme of hesitancy, uncertainty, and humility in the face of the divine call to be a prophet.

According to the Deuteronomistic tradition, Moses is considered to be the quintessential prophet. In Deuteronomy 18, where the law that governs prophecy is established, Moses says, "The Lord your God will raise up for you a prophet like me from your own people" (Deut 18:15). Moses is also depicted as a model prophet in the Pentateuchal narratives. When God encounters Moses for the first time at the burning bush (Exod 3:1–4:17), God commands him to go to Pharaoh with the divine message. Moses responds, "Who am I that I should go to Pharaoh, and bring the Israelites out of Egypt?" (Exod 3:11). In the same context Moses asks God what he should do if the people do not believe him (Exod 4:1), and later Moses claims that he is not an eloquent speaker, making reference to his "heavy tongue" (Exod 4:10). Much has been made about what exactly Moses meant by this remark. Did he have a speech impediment of some kind? Or is this mere hyperbole in the face of the gargantuan task of leading all of God's people out of

Egyptian slavery? It is, of course, impossible to know such details. At base Moses' words likely convey a humble reticence in light of the gravity of the task before him. Beyond the depiction of Moses' humility in his call narrative, his humble ways acquire legendary status and it is claimed that Moses is the most humble man on earth (Num 12:3). Pointing to Moses' humility while upholding him as the quintessential prophet in the biblical tradition underlines the importance of a humble stance when accepting the prophetic role.

The sixth-century BCE prophet Jeremiah provides an additional example of prophetic humility. Jeremiah was from a priestly family in Anathoth, a small town just a few miles north of Jerusalem. He witnessed the end of the Davidic monarchy when Nebuchadnezzar's Babylonian troops destroyed Jerusalem in 586 BCE. Years earlier, when Jeremiah was called by God, the prophet responded, "I do not know how to speak for I am only a youth" (Jer 1:6). The Hebrew word translated "youth" here is *na' ar*, which could refer to a boy of 12 or 13 or a young man of perhaps 20, or any age in between. While it is hard to know exactly what Jeremiah means by this term, it is unlikely that he was only 12 years old when God called him. It might even be the case that Jeremiah is older than a typical *na' ar*. Like Moses' reference to his "heavy tongue," Jeremiah's statement could be another example of hyperbole, employed in this context to suggest that he lacks the foundational sagely experience to speak to God's people on God's behalf. The wording suggests that Jeremiah is conveying real humility here, recognizing what a profound responsibility it is to become God's spokesperson. His attitude recalls the depiction of Moses, who, as noted above, also resisted God's call initially with claims of ineptitude. As in the case of Moses, we see in Jeremiah a kind of hesitancy that likely stems from uncertainty or humility.

Perhaps the most illuminating example of the call narrative appears in the book of Isaiah, an eighth-century prophet from Jerusalem who served the kings Ahaz and Hezekiah. Isaiah's humility is best seen when God encounters him near the beginning of his ministry through a vision depicting Yahweh's presence in the Temple. When Isaiah sees the divine presence in the sacred precinct

and the accompanying seraphim (fantastical, multi-winged crea-
tures), the prophet's first response is something like, "Oh no, I'm
in trouble." He goes on to confess, "I am a man of unclean lips and
I dwell among a people of unclean lips" (Isa 6:5). Precisely what
Isaiah means by this confession is elusive, as noted above about
Jeremiah's and Moses' responses to God. At the very least we see in
Isaiah a willingness to turn a critical eye upon himself and his own
people rather than standing aloof and condemning only others.
Isaiah seems to know his own limitations in this confession before
God. It is at this point when one of the seraphim touches Isaiah's
lips with a burning coal and proclaims, "Your guilt is taken away
and your sin is forgiven" (Isa 6:7). Isaiah's confession led to atonement by God. It is interesting to note that in the call narrative of
Jeremiah, God touches Jeremiah's mouth and tells him, "I have put
my words into your mouth" (Jer 1:9). Both prophets experience
the work of God directly in a physically similar vein as they begin
their prophetic ministry.

Isaiah's call narrative provides an important model for walking in the Old Testament prophetic tradition. Anyone who seeks
to see the world through the prophetic lens and wants to live a life
that bears witness to God's work in the world—in short, anyone
who wants to walk in the prophetic tradition—must start with the
same kind of introspective move. Among humans, no one possesses an entirely objective viewpoint and no one stands on the
perfect moral high ground. A person can respond to this notion of
flawed humanity in at least one of two ways. One response would
be something akin to despair, embodied in the point of view that
says, "I am not perfect and, therefore, I cannot call anyone else to
make good choices in life without feeling like a judgmental hypo-
crite." This option would lead to inaction and apathy toward the
problems of our world. This position is well represented in our
world today. The easiest thing for people to do—all people, Christian or not—is to be inactive and apathetic and then couch that
inactivity and apathy in a kind of hopeless humility.

A rather different option is expressed in the title of this book:
walking in the prophetic tradition. Rather than succumbing to

hopeless apathy, I am convinced that we can forge a way to live our lives in the prophetic tradition—remaining fully aware of our own faults and imperfections and yet still committing ourselves to live within the tension of calling others to live as God desires. This perspective is seen in Moses, Jeremiah, and Isaiah, and their response to God must be ours. We too must turn a critical eye on our own inability to live out God's ways perfectly. Yet our imperfection cannot paralyze us. Like these biblical prophets, we confess our failings and walk on. We admit that our lives, too, are an unfinished project as we call others to join our journey in the prophetic tradition. So like Moses, Jeremiah, and Isaiah, we speak the truth in love, calling others to change bad behavior and embrace the way of life God desires for us.

Even as we look to these biblical prophets as models for life in the prophetic tradition, I need to be clear about the difference between us and these ancient spokespersons for God. Unlike the biblical prophets, our words do not bear God's imprimatur—the divine stamp of approval—simply because we claim to be "walking in the prophetic tradition." I do not believe that God speaks to anyone today as God did to Moses, Jeremiah, Isaiah, or any of the other biblical prophets. So when we speak or bear witness to God's work in this world within the prophetic tradition, our words and our actions must be grounded in the testimony of the Bible in general and of the biblical prophets in particular. Anyone who wants to speak in the prophetic tradition always has the added burden of explaining how his or her words align with the biblical witness. Applying this criterion will forestall self-serving charlatans who are only attempting to control or manipulate people. From the perspective of this book, no one is free to create their own prophetic outlook apart from the biblical prophetic tradition.

MODERN VOICES

For a modern-day example of the kind of introspective sensibility Moses, Jeremiah, and Isaiah embody in the biblical tradition, I would point to each person I discuss in this book—Will Campbell,

Dorothy Day, Martin L. King Jr., Cornel West, César Chávez, and Myles Horton. Each of these individuals has expressed a profound willingness to look within himself or herself to see how they have not measured up to the kinds of standards to which they subscribe. In their writings and interviews, as well as in the personal testimonies of people who know or knew them, it is easy to see how they embody this basic prerequisite for a life within the prophetic tradition. The best examples in this group are Will Campbell, César Chávez, and Dorothy Day. I will introduce each of them here by giving brief overviews of their lives and then highlighting a few aspects of their experiences that vividly illustrate their humility.

Will Campbell (1924–2013) was a lifelong activist for justice and peace who was considered by many to be a renegade Christian preacher. Born and raised in Mississippi and in the Baptist Church, Campbell spent his life championing the cause of civil rights and serving as an advocate on behalf of the poor, and he was committed to reconciliation among all people. Campbell was the only white person invited by Martin L. King Jr. to help found the Southern Christian Leadership Conference in 1957. When the Little Rock Nine walked into Central High School on September 25 of that year in order to exercise their right to attend the school, Will Campbell walked with the group of students amidst the angry mob. Campbell was convinced that the institutions of church and university in the American South of the 1950s were too much at home in the world of Jim Crow segregation. Campbell was briefly employed by each (the Southern Baptist Convention and the University of Mississippi), but he soon realized that he could do more to champion civil rights and authentic Christianity by separating himself from those two institutions. Campbell has described the pivotal moments in his early life that enabled him to see the problems in the world around him.[9] As an Army medic in the South Pacific during World War II, he witnessed a young man being badly beaten by his French master for breaking an ashtray. He noted

9 Much of what follows in this section is taken from Campbell's own description of his experiences in Michael Letcher's documentary film *God's Will* (Tuscaloosa: University of Alabama Center for Public Television, 2000).

the similarity between that event and many like it back home in his native Mississippi, where the victims were African Americans. After the war Campbell returned home to pursue further education at Tulane, Wake Forest, and Yale Divinity School. He ended up working with the World Council of Churches in Nashville and dedicated his time and energy to enforcement of the 1954 *Brown v. Board of Education* ruling that outlawed segregation in public schools.

Yet for Campbell it was not enough to end the institutional aspects of racism. Campbell was also interested in personal reconciliation—helping people to learn how to forgive and see each other as human beings rather than representatives of warring constituencies. Campbell surprised many when he began reaching out to members of the KKK who were in prison. As a Southerner, Campbell was keenly aware of the ways in which the poor were manipulated by the racist powers that be in order to harass minorities. Campbell could see beyond the white robes and the hatred to the human beings who in some ways were a product of the society that shaped and used them. He believed that God's forgiveness was available for everyone—even racists. It is no surprise to discover that because of the stance he took on race and racism, Campbell was often reviled by people on both sides of the issue. Through his many books and lectures over the years Will Campbell has inspired numbers of people to work for civil rights for all people throughout the world. We will learn more about the specifics of Campbell's work in later chapters when we look at the prophetic themes of speaking truth to power and indicting the worship practices of Israel.

One expression of humility is the willingness to admit openly that one needs to change something about oneself. Campbell has written and spoken about a profound change of heart he experienced after the tragic death of Jonathan Daniels, a young seminarian who was killed while working in the civil rights struggle. This tragedy led Campbell to see that all people were recipients of God's love—victim and perpetrator alike. Campbell came to believe that he had wrongly assumed that commitment to the cause of civil rights required him to support the victims of discrimination and blame the perpetrators, drawing clear lines between the two. Yet after Daniels's death, he became convinced that God's love and redemption extends even to perpetrators, who are often caught in traps of their own making and are also in need of a way out. This point was chillingly brought home to Campbell by his good friend P. D. East, who had once asked Campbell to define Christianity in ten words or fewer. Campbell had responded, "We are all bastards but God loves us anyway."[10] Years later, as the community gathered together to mourn the loss of young Daniels, East came to Campbell and, referring to Daniels and the man who had murdered him, asked, "Which one of those bastards does God love more?" East was a former Christian who had trouble reconciling a loving God and the monstrous acts in human history. He was pushing Campbell to be consistent in his thinking while at the same time pointing out the difficulty in believing in God in the face of this tragedy. Reluctantly Will Campbell had to admit that according to his own understanding of God, both the victim and the perpetrator were loved by God equally. Campbell refers to this moment as the time when he began to rethink his role in reconciliation and race relations. For him, taking sides in this struggle was not a valid option. Working for reconciliation would demand understanding and compassion for perpetrator and victim alike.

César Estrada Chávez (1927–1993) was born in Yuma, Arizona, on his parents' farm, a homestead established by his grandfather in the 1880s. He lived there until the age of 10, when his family was evicted from their farm and forced to move to San Jose, California, where they lived in the barrio of Sal Si Puedes. Young César dropped out of school in the eighth grade and a few years later joined the US Navy. After his time in the service he returned to San Jose to work in the fields. By 1948 he had met, fallen in love with, and married Helen Fabela. In 1952 Chávez met a Catholic priest named Donald McDonnell who was committed to helping working people to negotiate with their employers. During the Great Depression, Congress passed the National Labor Relations

10. Campbell, *Brother to a Dragonfly*, 220.

Act of 1935, allowing workers to organize and collectively bargain with their employers. A later executive order, however, excluded farmworkers from this fundamental right. Correcting this exclusion became the goal of a number of activists after World War II. Father McDonnell was one of a number of priests who recognized the injustice in the exclusion of farm laborers, and he became a spiritual mentor for Chávez, introducing him to the history of the labor movement and encouraging him to become a leader for farmworkers in the area. Part of this informal tutelage included the teachings of Gandhi, especially his commitment to nonviolent direct action and noncooperation. As a lifelong Catholic, Chávez was taken with the notion of practicing labor relations within a Christian context. The moral and spiritual component of his vision for workers' rights brought a powerful unifying force to the United Farm Workers (UFW) movement and led many to believe in the eventual success of such a just cause. Chávez chose the Virgin of Guadelupe, the patron saint of Mexico, as a religious symbol for the movement and a natural rallying point for the UFW's faithful.[11] In later chapters we will have opportunity to explore in greater detail Chávez's role in critiquing empty religiosity and assisting working people and people trapped in poverty, and his willingness to speak truth to power on their behalf.

Chávez offers a model of humility in his practice of calling for fasting and repentance among his fellow workers even as they marched and led strikes against oppressive employers. He realized that hatred toward the oppressor and quests for revenge were destructive dead ends that must be avoided. His appropriation of the Christian idiom of loving one's enemy and the Christian practice of penance and repentance provided a way out of these traps for the farmworkers. Although the more secular members of the union were not always pleased with such appropriations of Christian tradition, Chávez sought to address through his faith and spiritual orientation what he believed was a deeper need beyond improved working conditions: a way to escape the violence that stems from hate. Marches were recast by Chávez as pilgrimages

11. Prouty, *César Chávez*, 24.

of repentance—repentance not simply on the part of the growers who were not treating the workers fairly, but on the part of the marchers as well, who, as human beings, needed to be contrite for their own imperfections. A 340-mile march from Delano, California, to Sacramento ended on Easter Sunday, and some observers wondered whether Chávez scheduled it to overlap with the penitential Lenten procession focused on prayer and atonement for past sins.[12] Additionally, fasting was implemented by Chávez as an expression of humility. Although fasting was used by Gandhi and others to draw public attention to injustice, Chávez recast the act as another mode of contrition and repentance. Surely not all marchers or even all who embraced the practice of fasting in the UFW embraced this Christian vision. Yet Chávez bore witness to the prophetic tradition of speaking the truth—even to oneself.

In addition to Will Campbell and César Chávez, Dorothy Day (1897–1980) provides an important model of humility in the modern prophetic tradition. Day was a lifelong activist on behalf of poor people, especially the working poor. She was the daughter of a journalist, which led to a rather peripatetic lifestyle during her childhood. Day was enamored with the ideals of socialism early in her life and resonated with the plight of working people. Day claims that her initial view of these concerns was profoundly shaped by Upton Sinclair's novel *The Jungle*, the story of an immigrant worker who fell prey to the excesses of the capitalist machine in the early years of the twentieth century. After dropping out of college she moved to New York City and followed in her father's footsteps, working as a reporter for the socialist paper *The Call*.

Growing increasingly comfortable with left-wing socialists and anarchists, the so-called "Lyrical Left," Day identified with rebels who eschewed Victorian sensibilities in favor of social and sexual experimentation. By 1917 she had served jail time for protesting alongside the suffragettes in Washington, DC. After numerous failed romantic relationships, one of which resulted in the birth of her daughter, Day became taken with Christianity and Roman Catholicism in particular. Her socialist and anarchist friends

12. Ibid., 28.

chided her for trying to be a socialist and a Catholic in the US at a time when those two viewpoints rarely converged. In preparation for an organized demonstration by unemployed laborers in Washington, DC, in December 1932, she convinced a Catholic newspaper, *The Commonweal*, to send her to cover the march. After the demonstration she prayed that God would open doors for her to use her talents to assist working people and especially the poor. When Day returned to New York, she met Peter Maurin and the two worked together to found *The Catholic Worker* in 1933. This publication sought to address the plight of working people using the resources of the Christian faith. In keeping with the ideals of the newspaper, Day and Maurin helped establish what they called "houses of hospitality" where poor people could find a hot meal, shelter, and fellowship with caring people.

Day worked with the poor and she lived with the poor. She spent her life calling Christians to live up to what they said they believed. In her newspaper she challenged the Catholic Church's position in labor disputes, drawing the ire of local church leaders in New York. Despite her willingness to expose the hypocrisy of the Catholic Church, she did not turn on the church in anger. As Day herself said, "I decided rather than hate the church I would pray for it." To illustrate the tension she felt, Day quoted the word of Father Romano Guardini, a twentieth-century Catholic priest: "The Church is the cross on which Christ was crucified; one could not separate Christ from his cross, and one must live in a state of permanent dissatisfaction with the Church."[13]

Day was well known for her pacifism, which was conspicuous at a time in US history when such a position was unwelcome in almost every major political and social circle. She refused to take sides in the Spanish Civil War when most US Catholics sided with the Nationalists under Franco. During World War II she and Peter Maurin established farms to allow people to work in a field other than industry or manufacturing in support of the war effort. Day remained committed to workers' concerns even into old age. She went to California to help César Chávez in the quest for

13. Day, *Long Loneliness*, 150.

better working conditions for farmworkers. Day was involved in the civil rights movement, riding buses to the American South to help with voter registration. In chapters 5 and 6 we will examine more details related to Dorothy Day's advocacy for working people and the poor. As one who was committed to speaking the truth through her newspaper and reaching out to those in need through her houses of hospitality, Day stands as a courageous witness to those who walk in the prophetic tradition.

Dorothy Day's humility can be grasped through her approach to heteronomy—a willingness to place one's self under the authority of another. In her day it was virtually impossible to identify oneself as a communist, socialist, and a Catholic at the same time. Faith in a god—any god—was anathema to most devoted communists and socialists in the early twentieth century. By submitting not just to the concept of belief in a god but to the Christian God, and indeed the Catholic depiction of that God, Dorothy Day appeared to many of her friends to be a walking contradiction. The kind of control that the Catholic Church represented in the history of Christendom made Day's commitment to the church seem almost comical to many of her friends. They would ask her how she could support what in their mind was one of the main sources of oppression of the world's people—especially disenfranchised working people. Yet Dorothy was unmoved. She submitted to the demands of the church, accepting its authority in her life. Such a stance amidst that kind of pressure from her peers is quite illustrative of the kind of humility Dorothy Day embodied. We have already noted some of the ways she wrestled with this tension regarding the power structures within the Catholic Church and will see further examples later. Yet her humility is manifested in her willingness to stay with the church, to pray for the church, rather than to dismiss it as so many of her friends did.

One additional mark of Dorothy Day's humility is a willingness to admit past mistakes. No one among the group of twentieth- and twenty-first-century voices we will examine in this book exhibits the level of deep confessional sensibility more than Dorothy Day. She is quite candid in her writings about the rather wild life she lived as a young person. She wrote about her bohemian experiences in her first novel, *The Eleventh Virgin*. Years later, after she had become a Christian, she went on a quest to locate and destroy every copy of the book because she had become so embarrassed by it. Part of her struggle during her "long loneliness," as she calls it, was to learn to forgive herself for her past life. The confessional life she lived and the humility that accompanied it was doubtless the source of the great well of compassion she exhibited toward all she encountered.

CONCLUSION

Humble introspection must be the starting point for everyone who walks in the prophetic tradition. No one likes being called to account by arrogant persons, such as Elmer Gantry, who denounce everyone around them without applying their own words to themselves. Moses, Jeremiah, and Isaiah provide us with tremendous biblical examples of people in the prophetic tradition who walked in humility before they began their prophetic work. Like these three prophets of old, Will Campbell, César Chávez, and Dorothy Day provide modern models of insight and humility, illustrating the foundational prerequisite for all who seek to journey within the prophetic tradition.

Call and obedience

2

Speaking Truth to Power

On June 5, 1989, the day after hundreds of Chinese citizens demanding democratic reform had been killed in the streets of Beijing by the Chinese army, one man brought an entire tank column to a halt in Tiananmen Square by simply standing in front of it—a lone human being face to face with military might. A photograph that appeared in many newspapers and other print media at that time showed a haunting image of bravery and resistance. Video footage of this man, now widely available, shows him matching the turns of the lead tank move for move until finally the tank stops. The man climbs onto the tank and appears to talk to the men inside for a period of time. After this interchange the man jumps down from the tank and assumes his position in front of the column again, matching every turn the lead tank makes. Many questions about that moment remain unanswered today. The Chinese government forbids discussion of "the June 4th incident" and no reliable official records indicate how many died in clashes with the army; likewise, the identity of this man and his fate remain unknown. Whatever this man's perspective on the student-led demonstrations and the previous day's massacre on the streets, it seems clear that he was determined to confront this tank column without any concern for his own safety. What is it about the image of this man standing in front of obviously superior weaponry that captures people's imagination? It is difficult to watch the video without a sense of profound admiration for this man's courage to confront authority. Perhaps no other image from the late twentieth century captures the spirit of the theme addressed in this chapter—speaking truth to power.

In this chapter we will examine people who, like this Chinese man, were willing to say what needed to be said to people who possessed power over others. In the Bible the prophets were often put in situations where they had to deliver a message from God that was not easy for people to hear—especially when the message was an indictment of royal behavior. These prophets had to muster the courage to speak this message and to rely on God's protection from the wrath that might result. In what follows I have gathered together the episodes where prophets speak a word of correction to persons in a position of power. Whether kings, priests, or military leaders are addressed, these prophetic encounters illustrate the prophetic mission to confront misguided power.

Some of the earliest examples of prophets speaking a truthful word from God to the king occur in the earliest days of the monarchy, during the reigns of Saul and David. In fact, it is no coincidence that the office of the prophet arises about the same time as kingship and that prophecy fades when the monarchy ends. The power vested in royalty needed divine checks and balances, and it seems that this corrective was delivered by the prophets who spoke to the kings. Many biblical scholars have suggested that the Old Testament prophetic tradition was primarily a spoken enterprise rather than a written one.[1] The earliest depictions of prophets portray them as spokespersons, as we will see below. Additionally, much of their discourse is introduced by the phrase "Thus says Yahweh," again, suggesting oral presentation. Thus although as readers we experience their interactions with powerful people as stories on the written page, we would do well to imagine their words as oral pronouncements. Thus, their spoken word encourages us to use our voices too in order to speak correction to abusive power today.

1. Birch, *Let Justice Roll Down*, 243.

The prophet Samuel is among the earliest prophets mentioned in the Old Testament. He is considered a transitional figure, since he is depicted as the last judge (1 Sam 7:15) and the first official prophet. He announces the appointment of the first Israelite king, Saul, but later condemns his behavior and announces the end of his reign.[2] Outside of a few stories from his childhood told in 1 Samuel, little is known about this early prophet. On one occasion when Saul gathered the people of Israel to fight against the Philistines (1 Sam 13:5–15), he was told by Samuel to wait for the prophet to offer a sacrifice before leading the army into battle. But Saul grew impatient and offered the sacrifice himself in Samuel's place, effectively usurping the prophetic role. When Samuel arrived and saw what Saul had done, the prophet rebuked the king and told him he had acted foolishly. Samuel further declared that Saul's kingdom would not continue.

After David became king, a prophet named Nathan appeared in his court. Little is known about his background. Nathan confronted David about his sin with Bathsheba (1 Sam 11–12). Nathan told David a story and entrapped the king with his own words. Nathan's story centered around a poor man who had a baby lamb that he raised as his own child. The poor man lived beside a wealthy man who had many flocks of sheep. One day the wealthy man had a guest and wanted to serve him a meal. Instead of using one of his many sheep, the wealthy man took the pet lamb from the poor man and served it to his guest. Nathan asked David what should be done to this wealthy man. David was outraged and declared that the wealthy man should die. In reply the prophet Nathan said to David, "You are the man." Nathan went on to expose the machinations that David had enacted and declared that God would punish him.

Years later after the monarchy had split into the northern tribes that retained the name Israel and a few southern tribes that formed the kingdom of Judah, an unnamed prophet from Judah

---

2. Samuel is portrayed in 1 Sam 9:9 as a "seer"—an old term for prophet according to this text. In 1 Chr 29:29 there is a reference to "the book of Samuel the seer," perhaps an old source the Chronicler used in his history.

confronted the altar in Bethel that had been established by Jeroboam I, the first ruler of the Northern Kingdom, sometime in
the late tenth century BCE (1 Kgs 13:1–10). Even though this unnamed prophet from Judah never directly accused Jeroboam, who
was present at Bethel that day, the king certainly understood the
implication of the prophet's message. Jeroboam's reaction to the
prophet, namely ordering his men to arrest him, demonstrates that
he knew that the prophet was speaking about him. Yet the prophet
walked away unharmed from this encounter with the king, showing the courage to speak truth even when threatened with arrest.

Jeroboam I was also challenged by a blind prophet named
Ahijah from Shiloh (1 Kgs 14:1–18), who spoke to him indirectly
through the king's wife. Some have speculated that his connections
to Shiloh might suggest that he was associated with priests, since
Shiloh was the early center of worship after the Israelites settled
in the land of Canaan. Jeroboam's wife comes to Ahijah and the
prophet tells her that disaster will befall their house—beginning
with the death of their son—because of Jeroboam's unfaithful ways.

The prophet Elijah is a central figure in 1–2 Kings, serving
as the primary divine spokesman to Ahab, king of Israel, who
reigned in the ninth century BCE. Elijah is one of the few prophets
in the Bible whose physical appearance is described. He is said to
be a "hairy man who wears a leather belt" (2 Kgs 1:8). Apparently
his looks were unique, since a later king named Ahaziah identified
him only by this description (2 Kgs 1:1–8). The prophet rebuked
King Ahab saying, "You and your father's house have troubled Israel because you have forsaken the commandments of God and
followed the Baals" (1 Kgs 18:17). Ahab's wife, the queen Jezebel,
had encouraged the worship of the Canaanite storm deity, Baal,
and Ahab had permitted it. True prophets were on the run at this
time in Israel because the crown had threatened them. Elijah himself had hidden many of these fugitive prophets in caves and sent
provisions to them during this persecution. Elijah's confrontation
with the king is the first of many encounters various prophets had
with Ahab.

Later an unnamed prophet came to King Ahab to rebuke him for disobedience to God (1 Kgs 20).[3] Disguising himself as one who had been wounded, the anonymous prophet approached Ahab and told the king a story about how he had lost a captive who had been placed under his care. The prophet told the king that he was forced to pay a talent of silver for losing the man, and he wanted the king to rule on this issue. The king of Israel ruled that the man in disguise should have to pay the penalty. The prophet immediately removed his fake bandages and told the king the same punishment would be applied to him, since he had freed a man whom Yahweh had decreed must die. This prophet trapped Ahab in the same way that Nathan caught David.

Ahab was confronted yet again by Elijah over the murder of Naboth and the theft of his vineyard. After the king's wife Jezebel hatched a plot to seize Naboth's land and have him killed, Ahab was rebuked by Elijah for "selling himself to do evil in the eyes of Yahweh" (1 Kgs 21:25).

Elijah also confronted Ahab's son, Ahaziah, who attempted to contact the deity named Baal Zebub of Ekron after suffering a serious injury from a fall in Samaria (2 Kgs 1). Elijah sent a message to the king, asking him if he was seeking a word from Baal Zebub because he assumed there was no God in Israel. Ahaziah responded by sending a small army to capture Elijah, with disastrous results: fire fell from the sky and destroyed the men (2 Kgs 1:9–12).

Elijah was succeeded by the prophet Elisha who literally carried on the prophetic mantle in ninth-century Israel. Elisha was a plowman, summoned by God to take the place of Elijah, who left only his outer cloak behind when he passed from this life (2 Kgs 2). Elisha spoke a word of rebuke to the king of Israel during the military campaign against Moab (2 Kgs 3:14). During the campaign the army's water supply dwindled, and the three kings who had combined their armies to fight against Moab sought out a prophet to advise them. When they found Elisha and asked him

3. Throughout this brief episode the king's name is not given. Its placement within the Ahab stories is the only basis for assuming that this is the proper name of the "king of Israel" in this prophetic encounter.

for advice, the prophet said to the king of Israel, "What have I to do with you? Go to the prophets of your father and the prophets of your mother" (2 Kgs 3:13), surely a prophetic jab at the apostasy of Ahab and Jezebel. Elisha continued by saying, "Were it not that I have respect for Jehoshaphat, the king of Judah, I would neither look at you nor see you" (2 Kgs 3:14) Eventually, however, Elisha relented and told the men that Yahweh would bring water for them.

Elisha also pronounced a word of doom to the captain of the Israelite army, who was close to the king (2 Kgs 7:2). During a siege of the city of Samaria many were growing desperate, and the king had sent to Elisha for advice. Elisha promised that all would return to normal the next day. The incredulous captain scoffed at this promise and questioned the prophet. Elisha assured him that it would indeed happen but that the captain would not live to see it. The prophetic word was carried out the next day when the captain was trampled to death at the city gate (2 Kgs 7:17).[4]

According to the Chronicler, the prophet Shemaiah rebuked Rehoboam, king of Judah (2 Chr 12:5). Although little is known about this prophet, the Chronicler cites a "Book of Shemaiah that tells about the kings of Israel. Because Rehoboam had abandoned God, Shemaiah declared that God would abandon him and his kingdom to Shishak, the Egyptian invader.

The eighth-century prophet Amos demonstrated a courageous willingness to confront the powers of his day over their deeds. Amos was a herdsman and vinedresser from Tekoah in Judah. God called him to journey to the Northern Kingdom of Israel to speak a word of correction there. On one occasion Amos told his audience, "I am not a prophet nor the son of a prophet" (Amos 7:14), admitting that he had no formal connection to professional

---

4. The final story of Elisha's confrontations with leaders is found in 2 Kgs 13:19, where he angrily rebukes Joash for not striking the ground with some arrows more than three times. Curiously, Elisha says to the king, "You should have struck the ground five or six times. Then you would have struck down the Arameans until you made an end of them. Now you will strike down Aram only three times." While this story indeed records a prophetic rebuke of a leader (and thus deserves mention in this chapter), it is unclear why such a harsh rebuke was given to the king at that moment.

prophets. God had simply called him from the midst of his work as a pastoralist and agriculturalist. Amos is unrivaled among biblical prophets for his biting critiques against a number of things—especially power. Amaziah, the priest of Bethel, accused the prophet of sedition against Jeroboam II, the king of Israel (Amos 7:10–17). After telling Amos to flee the region, Amaziah said, "Never again prophesy at Bethel, for it is the king's sanctuary, and it is a temple of the kingdom." Amaziah claimed that the worship site at Bethel was under royal hegemony. The implication seems to be that Amos needed the blessing of the crown to speak in that venue. Amos's response was cloaked in an indictment of that claim and its implications. The prophet argued that the divine prerogative, expressed in the command that was given to him as a spokesman for God, trumped the royal claims on the worship site. Amos went on to pronounce doom for Israel and for Amaziah's family.

Isaiah, another eighth-century prophet, rebuked Ahaz, king of Judah, for not asking God for a sign (Isa 7:10–17). Isaiah accused the king of wearying God with his refusal. Later the prophet Isaiah delivered a divine rebuke of Ahaz's son, King Hezekiah, after the king foolishly displayed the wealth of Jerusalem to Merodach-Baladan, the king of Babylon (Isa 39:1–2, 2 Kgs 20:12–18).

In the sixth century the prophet Jeremiah was imprisoned by courtiers of King Zedekiah (Jer 37:15). When the king came to visit Jeremiah, the prophet asked, "What wrong have I done to you or to your servants that you put me in prison?" (Jer 37:18). Before pronouncing doom on him and on Jerusalem, Jeremiah also asked the king about the false prophets who claimed that Babylon was no threat to Jerusalem (v. 19). It is little wonder that Jeremiah soon found himself cast into an empty cistern by the king's servants and left for dead (Jer 38:1–6).

The final prophetic encounter worthy of note here also took place during the days of Ahab and Elijah, but this time it was the prophet Micaiah, son of Imlah, who confronted the king (1 Kgs 22). I want to examine this story in greater detail since it illustrates the intricacies of the power dynamics that prophets faced when speaking the truth to kings. This is the only story about the prophet named Micaiah preserved in the Bible.[5] The story also introduces us to the false prophets with whom Ahab had surrounded himself—what we would call today "yes-men"—who could be counted on to tell the king what he wanted to hear.

One day, the kings of Israel and Judah, Ahab and Jehoshaphat, were discussing whether they should go to war against the Arameans. Jehoshaphat suggested that they consult God for advice, and so Ahab assembled his four hundred court prophets. They all spoke with one voice, encouraging Ahab and assuring him of success in battle. Yet the king of Judah, perhaps a little suspicious of this unanimous choir, wondered whether there were any other prophets of God to consult. Ahab replied that there was indeed one more prophet, Micaiah, but he hated Micaiah because he never had anything good to say to the king. By this statement, we are reminded of the ways many powerful people regard a biblical prophet, that is, a true prophet. Ahab hated Micaiah because true prophets often did not tell kings what they wanted to hear. The Judahite king, possessing a little more appreciation for the kind of prophet Micaiah exemplified, encouraged Ahab to summon him to appear before them.

As the two kings waited to hear from Micaiah, the yes-men prophets filled the king with every form of flattery for the coming military campaign. Meanwhile, the individual who was sent to bring Micaiah ben Imlah to Ahab greeted the prophet with an unsurprising word of advice—an encouragement to keep his message to the king positive. Pressure to agree with the yes-men was explicit in the messenger's words: "Let your words be like the words of the other prophets" (v. 13). Yet Micaiah was no ideological mercenary for the crown. He was no court-prophet yes-man. He claimed to speak only what God told him.

Curiously, the message Micaiah received from God centered on deception: Micaiah was instructed to deceive the king by agreeing with the yes-men who were predicting success. People of faith are sometimes bothered by the ethics of God commanding a true prophet to lie. Whether that should be a problem for us in this

---

5. See a parallel account of this story in 2 Chronicles 18.

story is a topic I leave to others. For our purposes it is interesting to read what happens after Micaiah declared to Ahab, "Go up and be successful" (v. 15). The king of Israel said, "How many times do I have to make you swear to tell me nothing but the truth?" (v. 16). In his response we see some indication that both kings knew that Micaiah was not being fully transparent about this divine word. Perhaps Micaiah delivered his message in a sarcastic tone or gave some nonverbal cue that his words were not meant to be taken seriously. In any case, it is clear from the context that at least one of the kings knew he was not speaking the truth. At this point Micaiah proclaimed the true word of God: Israel would be scattered like sheep with no shepherd, and its leaders—presumably the kings of Israel and Judah—would not return to their homes in peace. His message enraged the king of Israel and prompted him to remind the king of Judah that this result was exactly what he anticipated from this renegade prophet. Micaiah then revealed what had transpired in Yahweh's heavenly court when the deity sought someone to deceive the king of Israel. A lying spirit volunteered to put deceptive words in the mouths of the court prophets, said Micaiah, in order to entice Ahab to attack at Ramoth Gilead so that he would die in the battle.

At this point one of the yes-men prophets, Zedekiah, came forward and struck Micaiah for what he surely perceived to be an act of insolence toward the king. Zedekiah asked his opponent, "By which way did the spirit of Yahweh cross over from me to you?" (v. 24)—a witty retort to accompany the punch to Micaiah's face. Ahab then ordered the arrest of Micaiah and instructed his men to hold him in prison until the king returned "in peace." As he was being hauled off to his cell Micaiah said to Ahab, "If you return in peace, Yahweh has not spoken through me" (v. 28).

Ahab, of course, dies in the battle at Ramoth Gilead. The biblical narrator reports that even though the king tried to disguise himself on the battlefield, he was nevertheless killed—by a misfired arrow. So Micaiah was proven right and the king returned home to be buried.

This biblical story has much to teach us. First, in Ahab's four hundred prophets it provides a clear illustration of what we are calling "yes-men"—people who simply say what powerful people want to hear. These prophets of the king were there to provide a rubber-stamped affirmation for what the king of Israel wanted. Although these men are called prophets in this episode, from the biblical point of view these prophets are actually false prophets. Thus, this story should serve as a cautionary tale about prophets who actually are mere yes-men. Most people have little difficulty imagining a modern-day version of these prophets that surrounded King Ahab. Sycophantic people seem never to be too far away from any context where power is wielded. This story portrays them as the opposite of the true prophet, Micaiah, the one who has the courage to tell the kings the truth. The interaction between Ahab and Micaiah serves as a warning to readers regarding the danger of listening to people who pretend to walk in the prophetic tradition but are actually not prophets at all. Modern people who seek to walk in the prophetic tradition have to be aware of the yes-men and yes-women who may exist in any social system—society at large, businesses, churches, schools, community organizations, or extended families.

Second, the story of Micaiah illustrates a courageous prophet willing to speak the word of God to the leaders of his day amidst the sycophantic voices who surround the king's throne. Micaiah's refusal to succumb to the pressure of the courtiers and the chorus of yes-men "prophets" must have taken tremendous courage. Additionally, this pressure was physical as well as ideological, as the court prophet's act of striking Micaiah makes clear. The story upholds this kind of courageous resistance and serves as a model for those today who seek to walk in this same tradition.

We must also be introspective about our own potential to become yes-men and yes-women. Those who wish to walk in the prophetic tradition must ask themselves, "Do we speak our words so that the people in power will like us and include us?" The courageous example of Micaiah must direct our journey, encouraging us to speak truth to those in power, from the heads of small organizations to the leaders who wield great authority over others. Micaiah's story is a warning to those inclined to be yes-men and yes-women. It is also a call to walk courageously in the prophetic tradition and speak truth to power.

MARTIN L. KING JR.

Speaking truth to power in the twentieth-century American context is in many ways epitomized by Dr. Martin Luther King Jr. King was born in Atlanta, Georgia. His father, Martin Luther King Sr., was a minister at the Ebenezer Baptist Church in Atlanta and his mother, Alberta Williams King, played the piano for the church and served in a number of leadership capacities among the women of the congregation. The younger Martin King graduated from Morehouse College and Crozer Theological Seminary and went on to earn a Ph.D. from Boston University. He was propelled to the national spotlight during the Montgomery Bus Boycott of 1955–56. King had been elected head of the Montgomery Improvement Association just days after Rosa Parks was arrested for refusing to relinquish her seat in keeping with the city's segregation laws. King went on to become one of the founders of the Southern Christian Leadership Conference in 1957.

Throughout the 1960s King was at the forefront of a number of efforts to confront segregation laws. He helped organize sit-ins in Atlanta and in Albany, Georgia, as well as demonstrations in Birmingham and Selma, Alabama, and St. Augustine, Florida. Imprisoned numerous times for civil disobedience, King experienced firsthand the violence imposed in defense of the Jim Crow segregation system. For his work King was awarded the 1964 Nobel Peace Prize, and throughout his life he traveled the world speaking with eloquence and grace, calling for an end to racial inequality. In addition to working for civil rights for African Americans, King also spoke out against the Vietnam War and the unfair treatment of municipal sanitation workers in Memphis. In the end King gave his life for the cause of civil rights. He survived numerous death threats, and even direct attempts on his life. King spoke truth to power in love perhaps better than any other twentieth-century activist. His death at the hands of an assassin in Memphis, Tennessee, on April 4, 1968, demonstrated just how dangerous truth-telling and standing for justice can be in a world determined not to hear it.

King's commitment to speak truth to power was illustrated on numerous occasions in his life. As a young man he was tasked with leading the effort to desegregate the Montgomery, Alabama, bus system. In that endeavor King was pitted against the powers of the city government in Montgomery. After being arrested in Birmingham, Alabama, for unlawful protest, King wrote a letter from his jail cell to the moderate clergymen who had called for him to slow down the efforts for equality. King stood against the Alabama authorities too: Bull Connor, Birmingham's commissioner of public safety, and his water cannons, as well as the state's governor, George Wallace, and the Alabama State Police at the Edmund Pettus Bridge.

Against the city of Birmingham King said,

> Birmingham is probably the most thoroughly segregated city in the United States. Its ugly record of police brutality is known in every section of this country. Its unjust treatment of Negroes in the courts is a notorious reality. There have been more unsolved bombings of Negro homes and churches in Birmingham than any city in this nation. These are the hard, brutal and unbelievable facts. On the basis of these conditions Negro leaders sought to negotiate with the city fathers. But the political leaders consistently refused to engage in good faith negotiation.[6]

In his last speech before he was cut down by a sniper's bullet, King spoke truth to power as he reflected on his confrontation with Bull Connor.

> I remember in Birmingham, Alabama, when we were in that majestic struggle there, we would move out of the 16th Street Baptist Church day after day: by the hundreds we would move out. And Bull Connor would

6. King, "Letter from Birmingham City Jail," 290.

tell them to send the dogs forth and they did come; but we just went before the dogs singing, "Ain't gonna let nobody turn me around." Bull Connor next would say, "Turn the fire hoses on." And as I said to you the other night, Bull Connor did not know history. He knew a kind of physics that somehow didn't relate to the transphysics that we knew about. And that was the fact that there was a certain kind of fire that no water could put out.... That couldn't stop us. And we just went before the dogs and we would look at them and we'd go on before the water hoses and we would look at it, and we'd just go on singing "Over my head I see freedom in the air." And then we would be thrown in the paddy wagons, and sometimes we were stacked in there like sardines in a can. And they would throw us in, and old Bull would say, "Take them off," and they did; and we would just go on in the paddy wagon singing, "We Shall Overcome." And every now and then we'd get in the jail, and we'd see the jailers looking through the windows being moved by our prayers, and being moved by our words and our songs. And there was a power there which Bull Connor couldn't adjust to; and so we ended up transforming Bull into a steer, and we won our struggle in Birmingham.[7]

King's response to Governor Wallace's statement "Segregation today, segregation tomorrow, segregation forever" was recorded in an interview published in *Playboy* magazine.

Governor Wallace is a demagogue with a capital D. He symbolizes in this country many of the evils that were alive in Hitler's Germany. He is a merchant of racism, peddling hate under the guise of states' rights. He wants to turn back the clock, for his own personal aggrandizement, and he will do literally *anything* to accomplish this. He represents the misuse, the corruption, the destruction of leadership. I am not sure that he believes all the poison that he preaches, but he is artful enough to convince others that he does. Instead of guiding people to new peaks of reasonableness, he intensifies misunderstanding,

7. King, "I See the Promised Land," 281–82.

deepens suspicion and prejudice. He is perhaps the most dangerous racist in America today.[8]

After the bloody encounter on the Edmund Pettus Bridge on March 7, 1965, King planned to resume the march to expose the vicious racism in the state of Alabama from the governor's office all the way down to the sheriff's office in the city of Selma. Acting against the governor's order to cancel the march and the injunction set forth by Judge Frank M. Johnson from the federal district court in Montgomery, King marched on with these words:

> As a matter of conscience I felt it was necessary to seek a confrontation with injustice on Highway 80 [the road that crossed the Edmund Pettus Bridge in Selma], I asked them to try to understand that I would rather die on the highway in Alabama than make a butchery of my conscience by compromising with evil. The Reverend Fred Shuttlesworth said to the Governor that instead of urging us not to march, he should urge the state troopers not to be brutal toward us and not attempt to stop our peaceful march.[9]

These are but a few of the many ways Martin King spoke truth to power during his lifetime. His was a powerful voice, but his willingness to embody his words in the face of all the obstacles of hate and discrimination in the US gave those words even greater power. King's courage to stand for what is right and his commitment to speaking the truth to power clearly qualify him to serve as a paragon of the living, breathing prophetic tradition in twentieth-century America.

CÉSAR CHÁVEZ

When César Chávez confronted the grape growers in Delano, California, and organized the United Farm Workers in 1962 in order to protest working conditions, he knew firsthand what it

8. King, "*Playboy* Interview," 373.
9. King, "Behind the Selma March," 130.

meant to speak truth to power. He had gone to Oxnard, California, in 1958 to see the *bracero* program in action. This program was a solution the federal government had created to address a shortage of farmworkers during World War II by using taxpayer money to import laborers from Mexico. Despite its early success during the war, the *bracero* program was manipulated by growers to keep wages low and workers tightly controlled. Although the workers were free to leave the farm at any time, they could be deported back to Mexico if they were not employed. Through the 1950s the system was further abused by the growers, who brought in more workers than were needed. The surplus meant that workers were competing for work and thus not inclined to complain about poor working conditions. After witnessing the corruption Chávez organized a sitdown strike at farms that were abusing the *bracero* program. The growers were outraged by these strikes, and agribusiness took notice of the audacity of this new threat to their profits—César Chávez. His willingness to confront the powerful owners led others to call attention to other abuses, and eventually the *bracero* program was brought to an end. His work at Oxnard laid the foundation for speaking the truth on behalf of exploited workers at Delano years later. The march he led from the heart of the grape-growing region in California to the state capital constituted the most important statement to the powers of agribusiness on behalf of farmworkers to that point. The strike that followed unmasked the farm laborers' deplorable working conditions and displayed the way they were being exploited by the grape-growing industry.

Chávez's commitment to stand up on behalf of the workers in the face of the powerful California agribusiness took courage and strength. His telling the truth about the abuses of the *bracero* program and organizing people to stand against it is another good example of speaking truth to power within the trajectory of the Old Testament prophetic tradition.

WILL CAMPBELL

Like King and Chávez, Will Campbell knew what it was like to speak the truth to the world around him, and he also knew the price of that stance. As one of the great southern voices in the civil rights movement and a radical Christian preacher, Campbell constitutes a fitting example of one who walked in the prophetic tradition and provides an interesting modern parallel to Micaiah ben Imlah.

The legacy of Micaiah is easy to spot in an essay Will Campbell coauthored with James Y. Holloway as an open letter to Billy Graham during the Vietnam War, appearing originally in the journal *Katallagete*, a publication Campbell helped found.[10] In this open letter Campbell chastises evangelist and fellow Baptist Billy Graham for being a yes-man, not unlike the prophets that surrounded Ahab in the story of Micaiah. Campbell asks Graham why he looked so much like the figure Zedekiah son of Kenaanah, the court prophet who lent his blessing and influence to the kings of Israel and Judah in the biblical story we examined above. Campbell suggested that Graham had allowed himself to be courted too much by the powers that be. Graham had been drawn into political maneuvers on the national stage, becoming close with US presidents Lyndon Johnson and Richard Nixon, as well as candidates for that office such as George Wallace.

Billy Graham's close ties to the Nixon presidency have been well documented. On May 28, 1970, Nixon made an appearance on the stage at one of Graham's crusade rallies at Neyland Stadium on the campus of the University of Tennessee in Knoxville. A few weeks earlier, on May 4, Ohio National Guard troops had fired on student protesters at Kent State University, killing four and wounding nine, and there was widespread dissent among students and faculty at many universities throughout the country regarding Nixon's policy in Vietnam. Nixon's appearance at Graham's

---

10. Campbell and Holloway, "Open Letter to Dr. Billy Graham." *Katallagete* (the title derives from the Greek word meaning "be reconciled," 2 Cor 5:20) was published by the Committee of Southern Churchmen.

crusade was seen by many to be a convenient way for Nixon to give the appearance of being welcome on a university campus in the wake of the Kent State shootings. Campbell concluded his letter by suggesting that the best way Graham could minister to the US soldiers in Vietnam as well as the Vietnamese people as a whole was to prophesy to the Pentagon and White House in the tradition of Micaiah, son of Imlah.

Campbell's opposition to the war in Vietnam was by no means unique in 1971. But his words as a churchman to the popular Billy Graham were not welcomed by most Christians in general, and certainly not most Southern Baptists in particular. Yet the passage of time allows us to see Campbell's words to Graham in a new light, a light that illuminates their wisdom. Like Micaiah, Will Campbell had the courage to speak the right word even if it meant being ostracized by most people in that day. True, Campbell did not face imprisonment over his words as Micaiah and King did. Yet his courage to speak out cost Campbell greatly within Baptist circles.

This was not the only time Campbell had harsh words for Billy Graham. In 1973 Campbell and his partner at the journal *Katallagete* wrote a piece called, "Can There Be a Crusade for Christ?"[11] In this article Campbell questioned the programs that Graham labeled "crusades" and noted how easily spreading the Christian Gospel can become a process of conquering people in order to advance one's own causes. Treating the proclamation of the Christian Gospel as a crusade set up an us-versus-them mentality and encouraged notions of conquest and victory. Campbell called all of these assumptions into question and asserted, "The gospel [literally "good news"] does not concern what most of us want to hear about good news, namely something advancing our causes." He pointed to the worst forms of such abuses in Christendom's crusades against Muslims and, later, against native peoples in North America, as well as the crusades against indigenous peoples led by Christian mission efforts all over the world. For Campbell, political maneuvering by Christian leaders was simply

11. Campbell, "Crusade for Christ," 128–33.

another page in a long history of people using Christianity as a mode of advancing some other agenda. In his essay Campbell singled out Billy Graham and the Quaker president Richard Nixon as examples of this crusader mentality that he claimed is foreign to the good news of Jesus Christ.

For a final example we turn to Will Campbell speaking a critique by refusing to cooperate with the authorities in the Tennessee state prison system. In January 1973 Campbell received a letter from one of the state prison chaplains, Amos Wilson, who informed Campbell that one of the men from the Committee of Southern Churchmen, a prison ministry with which Campbell was affiliated, did not meet with the chaplain's approval. Wilson also expressed concern for the minister's openness to working with inmates whom the chaplain deemed too pathological to reform. Campbell responded to Wilson by saying that he could not answer for the man in question but he would be happy to sit down to discuss the matter with the chaplain.[12] Campbell said that as a Christian he had no interest in assisting the state's agenda in the prisons. Campbell claimed that he was there to assist the prisoners who wanted his help. The needs and desires of the state were of no concern to him or to anyone else in the prison ministry. Further, the state's identification of prisoners as too pathological to reform was, from Campbell's point of view, a label that Christian ministers simply did not recognize because of their Christian commitment. For Campbell no one was "too pathological" to change their ways. Campbell's actions in this matter further illustrate his willingness to speak truth to the people in power, demonstrating his commitment to walking in the prophetic tradition of Samuel, Nathan, Elijah, Elisha, and Micaiah.

CONCLUSION

There is a subtle temptation when speaking truth to power to blur the lines between speaking on behalf of others and speaking on

12. Campbell, "Exchange of Letters," 26–30.

behalf of one's own desires. The biblical prophets were endowed by God to approach their confrontations with power properly, in keeping with God's will. The twentieth-century voices we have examined in this chapter were clearly committed to advocacy for others. Martin King acted on behalf of African Americans in the US. César Chávez spoke the truth in defense of agricultural workers in California. Will Campbell stood for those being victimized by the Vietnam War and those in the US prison system and critiqued the conquest-minded approach endorsed by his fellow Baptists. As we noted in chapter 1, the prophetic tradition must begin with a self-critical stance, a humility that seeks to avoid self-centered acts. Determining when to raise our voices against the powers that be is a foundational step in support of those in need, rooted in the tradition of Christian spiritual discernment. The biblical models and those who walk in the prophetic tradition in our own age point the way. Speaking truth to power in the biblical tradition takes profound courage. The numerous episodes from the lives of the prophets we examined in this chapter continue to provide guidance for those who seek it. That tradition continues in the pronouncements of Martin Luther King Jr., César Chávez, and Will Campbell, twentieth-century voices who can inspire us all today.

3

Prophets as Transparent Historians

MOST CULTURES OF THE world have ways of covering up mistakes from their past. In the American context the usual approach is simply to ignore unpleasant moments in our collective history; if we do not speak of those events, so the thinking goes, perhaps they will somehow vanish from the historical record. Other cultures have been a little more heavy-handed in dealing with past missteps. Take, for example, the communist approach in Czechoslovakia during the Cold War. In his novel *The Book of Laughter and Forgetting*, Milan Kundera writes about Vladimír Clementis, who was a communist leader in 1948 when his communist comrade Klement Gottwald took over in what was known as the "Victorious February" coup d'etat. Clementis and Gottwald were photographed on a balcony in Prague, a picture that became quite famous throughout the country, symbolizing the complete communist takeover. As Kundera notes, "every child knew the photograph from posters, schoolbooks, and museums."

In the photo, taken on a cold day, Gottwald is wearing a hat that actually belonged to Clementis, who had loaned it to Gottwald just before the picture was taken. Clementis eventually fell out of favor with the communists, however, and was hanged for treason in 1952. The communist authorities, wishing to distance themselves from the condemned man, edited the photograph and airbrushed Clementis out, leaving President Gottwald alone on the balcony. For decades only the airbrushed version was repro- duced. A careful analysis of the original photograph and the edited copy reveals that the microphones on stands in front of the men were shifted closer to Gottwald so that Clementis's face was totally covered. A photographer who in the original image appeared be- hind both men on the balcony was completely removed from the retouched photograph. The only vestige of Clementis's presence on the balcony that cold February day was the hat that Gottwald wore.

The impulse to correct history's mistakes, whether personal or national, is all too common among humans.[1] Yet we gener- ally recognize the dishonesty of attempts at whitewashing the past. Although it might be difficult for us to be critical of our own par- ticipation in this practice of plastering over the mistakes we, our family, or our nation have made, we are able to recognize it when others do it. When we see this at work in other cultures, it feels natural to accuse them of dishonesty—even when the accusation might be somewhat hypocritical. An honest accounting of our- selves as human beings would require us to admit just how strong the impulse is within us to cover over past mistakes. This persistent pattern of concealment is what makes the Old Testament stand out within world literature as a rather transparent account of a people's past. There is a deep level of candor among the biblical writers in general and several of the prophets in particular. In this chapter we will examine the theme of prophetic transparency and its impor- tant contribution to the prophetic tradition.

There are two prophets who stand out for their truth-telling within the Old Testament prophetic tradition: Hosea and Jeremi- ah. Although they lived centuries apart, both prophets possessed a willingness to remind Israel of the infelicities of their collective past. Thus we might think of them as prophetic historians who combined the courage to speak the truth, demonstrated by the

---

1. Much of this chapter is based upon my article "Cornel West, Biblical Transparency, and American Historical Amnesia," *Theology Today* 68 (2011): 123–33. Used with permission.

prophets we examined in the previous chapter, with a determination to remind the people of Israel of their past. Within the books that bear their names, the prophets Hosea and Jeremiah dared to expose the sins and mistakes of their people's history. The concern for deep introspection and transparency common to the work of these two prophets and one modern voice, Cornel West, is the subject of this chapter.

HOSEA

During the eighth century BCE the prophet Hosea was active in the northern kingdom of Israel. His work seems to have begun sometime during the reign of King Jeroboam II (786–746 BCE), and it is likely to have ended before the destruction of Samaria in 721 BCE. The timing of Hosea's career is significant because it provides an early glimpse of a transparent accounting of the past almost two centuries before the Babylonian exile in 586 BCE, and thus demonstrates the chronological depth of this important prophetic theme.

The aspect of Hosea's life that is highlighted by most interpreters and theologians is the prophet's marriage to a prostitute. Hosea was commanded by God to marry a prostitute named Gomer to illustrate the fractured and troubled relationship God had with Israel. This is indeed a powerful component of the book of Hosea. However, another facet of Hosea's message that has received less attention is profoundly important for people of faith today—the importance of the past.

There are a number of passages in the book of Hosea that refer to Israel's past, and these references are not simply nostalgic remembrances. Hosea referred to moments in Israel's past that were far from joyous and pleasing. The book begins with a historical allusion to the shedding of blood in the Valley of Jezreel. The prophet was instructed by Yahweh to name his firstborn son Jezreel because Yahweh planned to punish the dynasty of Jehu for the blood of Jezreel (Hos 1:4). A fuller account of Jehu's bloodshed is provided in 2 Kgs 9, where Jehu was anointed by an unnamed prophet sent by the prophet Elisha and instructed to strike down the dynasty of Ahab, a task he carried out with murderous zeal. Jehu killed King Joram (a.k.a. Jehoram) near Naboth's vineyard, the plot of ground that Ahab and Jezebel had illegally seized after arranging Naboth's death (2 Kgs 9:24). Jehu instructed his servant to dump Joram's body on this same plot of ground located in the valley of Jezreel. But Jehu also killed the Judahite king Ahaziah, who was visiting Joram. Perhaps Jehu chose to eliminate him because Ahaziah's maternal grandmother was Jezebel, the wife of Ahab. Jehu then entered the city of Jezreel and had Jezebel murdered too (2 Kgs 9:30–33). Jehu's violent campaign in the valley of Jezreel culminated in a massive slaughter. Jehu assembled the sons of Ahab, had them all killed, and ordered that their heads be sent to Jezreel and put on display for all to see (2 Kgs 10:1–11).

The book of Hosea reveals that Yahweh did not intend the destruction to go as far as Jehu took it. As a result, Yahweh told Hosea that the dynasty of Jehu would suffer for this excess. Hosea's audience no doubt recognized the connection between the child's name and the violent history of Jehu's rampage. This allusion to the events outlined in 2 Kgs 9–10 is the first of several historical references in Hosea.

In the second historical allusion God said to Israel, "I will make the Valley of Achor a door of hope" (Hos 2:15 [Hebrew 2:17]). In the passage that contains this promise, God made reference to the time Israel spent in the wilderness after coming out of the land of Egypt. So it seems quite likely that the reference to the Valley of Achor could easily be a cipher for the events centered around Achan, also known as Achor (1 Chr 2:7). This man violated the ban on plunder following the destruction of Jericho, which marked the beginning of Joshua's conquest of Canaan (Josh 7:16–26). After the battle, it was discovered that someone had taken some of the spoils, in violation of the command of God. As the book of Joshua recounts, the sin of Achan prevented Israel from being victorious when they assaulted the city of Ai. After Achan was identified as the guilty party, he and his family were executed by stoning and were buried in the Valley of Achor. Just as the events of Jehu's bloody rampage could not be separated from their setting in the valley of Jezreel, the crime of Achan was evoked by Hosea's allusion to the Valley of Achor. Each episode was profoundly memorable for Israel, to the extent that a brief geographical reference would call to mind a tragedy that led to collective hardship.

Hosea referred to this tragic event from Israel's collective history to illustrate God's ability to overturn the destructive past in a hopeful vision. A site of shame would one day become a door of hope. On this occasion, Hosea cited Israel's history to remind them of a difficult moment, but that memory, he asserted, would be replaced by a better one.

On two separate occasions the book of Hosea cites "the days of Gibeah" as a synonym for bad behavior. First, Hosea spoke of the sinfulness of Israel and declared, "They have deeply corrupted themselves as in the days of Gibeah" (9:9). In the following chapter God said to the people of Israel, "From the days of Gibeah you have sinned O Israel" (10:9). While the city of Gibeah appears in a number of biblical stories, the event to which Hosea most likely referred is recounted in the grim tale of Judg 19. A Levite pursued his concubine to the house of her father after some incident that prompted her departure.[2] The Levite convinced her to return home with him and on their journey they stopped at Gibeah for the night. Although they were invited into a local man's home, the house was later surrounded by a gang of rapists. The Levite's concubine was handed over to the gang, who brutally raped and murdered her. This outrage led to a civil war within the tribes of Israel, narrated in Judg 20. The horrific nature of the incident at Gibeah and the intertribal conflict it precipitated likely made it a memorable event even centuries later.[3] Hosea summoned up this

2. The MT suggests that she was sexually unfaithful to the Levite. One of the Septuagint versions of this story simply says the concubine became angry with the Levite, a version that appears to me to be more likely. See Jason Bembry, "The Levite's Concubine."

3. One additional way this theme of the prophetic use of history assists our understanding of Israel's traditions surrounds the writing of history itself. Some scholars have suggested that the book of Judges has little basis in real history and is merely an ideologically motivated collection of tales designed

event with a phrase that his hearers would immediately associate with the brutal acts narrated in Judg 19. His shorthand allusion was a poignant reminder that the sinfulness current in Hosea's day is reminiscent of a great tragedy in Israel's collective past.

In a final reference to Israel's former days, Hosea brought up the incident at Baal Peor as an example of historic unfaithfulness (9:10). Hosea likely referred to the story recounted in Num 25:1–16, although it is not clear which of the details of that story Hosea had in mind. The prophet simply said, "But they entered Baal Peor and consecrated themselves to Baal and became disgusting things like the thing they loved." Numbers 25 is an account of Israel's unfaithfulness to Yahweh just as they are about to enter the land of Canaan. The story as it now stands seems to be a patchwork of pentateuchal sources, combining a story of Israel "playing the harlot" with the daughters of Moab and making offerings to their gods with a story of improper sexual activity between an Israelite man and a Midianite woman. While we cannot trace here the threads in the redactional tapestry of this story, it is clear that what happened at Baal Peor was a disappointment to Yahweh because it involved worshiping another deity. Like the references to Jezreel, the valley of Achor, and "the days of Gibeah," the allusion to Baal Peor is a further indication that Hosea operates as a prophetic historian, reminding Israel of their long history of unfaithfulness to Yahweh.

JEREMIAH

The eighth-century BCE prophet Hosea is not the only biblical prophet who referred to Israel's past as a way to call them to think about the present. Jeremiah, who was active for several decades during the seventh and sixth century, employed a similar tactic in

---

to serve political ends. For this point of view see Brettler, "Book of Judges." It seems to me that Hosea's appropriation of place names that connect to these tragic stories militates against Brettler's argument. If Hosea's references have no basis in history, the rhetorical force of his words is reduced to virtually nothing.

his message to the people of Jerusalem, just before the Babylonian army advanced and destroyed the beloved capital city.

In the so-called Temple Sermon that is recorded in Jer 7 and perhaps repeated in Jer 26, the prophet called the people to mend their ways and do God's will by seeking justice, avoiding oppression of the marginalized, refusing to shed innocent blood, and refraining from worshiping idols. Jeremiah chided the people for trusting in what appears to be some sort of protective mantra: "This is the Temple of Yahweh" (Jer 7:4). Many people were apparently persuaded that Yahweh's temple in Jerusalem was unassailable. Perhaps this ideology was rooted in the days of Hezekiah, when the Assyrian army under Sennacherib surrounded Jerusalem but did not destroy it; neither did they remove Hezekiah from his throne. Even the Assyrian annals admit these facts.[4] Such an accomplishment by Hezekiah, a political lightweight vis-à-vis the mighty Assyrian army, led many of the inhabitants of Jerusalem to believe that there was something special about their city. They were convinced that Jerusalem was protected by their God and thus could never be vanquished. A century or so later "the Temple of Yahweh" became a slogan whereby the people affirmed their God's power to protect Jerusalem from invaders. Yet Jeremiah chided the crowd on the Temple mount for trusting in what he called "deceptive words."

To challenge those who put their faith in the mantra, Jeremiah suggested that whoever trusts in the protection of the Jerusalem Temple should go to Shiloh. His advice was likely an allusion to the shrine that the Israelites established there in the early days of their settlement in the land of Canaan. Although the biblical testimony does not indicate exactly what kind of structure stood at Shiloh in those early days, 1 Sam 1–4 provides a glimpse into that past, allowing us to elucidate the point Jeremiah sought to make with his audience. In the narrative world of the Old Testament, Shiloh became the worship center of Israel after Joshua led the people into Canaan. At Shiloh was housed the ark of the covenant and perhaps

---

4. See the inscription on the Oriental Institute Prism of Sennacherib in Pritchard, *Ancient Near Eastern Texts*, 288.

what remained of the tent of meeting or tabernacle, the moveable shrine used by Israel in the wilderness. No biblical narrative provides a clear explanation of how the shrine at Shiloh was arranged.

According to 1 Samuel, the priest Eli and his sons were overseeing worship activities in this locale. It was at Shiloh that Hannah vowed to give her child, Samuel, to God. As the Israelites, encamped at Ebenezer, prepared to face the army of the Philistines near Aphek, the elders of Israel suggested that the ark of the covenant be carried into battle, as a way to ensure victory. The battle took place between Ebenezer (the Israelite camp) and Aphek (the Philistine camp). Despite the presence of the ark within the armies of Israel, the battle belonged to the Philistines that day. Eli's sons, Hophni and Phineas, were killed and the ark of the covenant was captured by the Philistines and carried off to their territory. When the news of the defeat reached Shiloh, the people's hopes were shattered. Upon hearing of the death of his sons and the loss of the ark, Eli fell over backwards, broke his neck, and died. When Phineas's wife learned of her husband's death, she went into labor, gave birth, and she too died (1 Sam 4:18–20).

At this point in the narrative the scene shifts to the Philistine cities where the ark had been taken by its captors, and nothing more is heard of Shiloh in the books of Samuel. Yet circumstantial evidence suggests there was more to the story. First, the Old Testament never again mentions Shiloh as a center for worship in Israel. By the time of Saul the priests were centered on the city of Nob, near Jerusalem (1 Sam 21:2). We might, therefore, infer from this particular silence that after capturing the ark the Philistines pursued the retreating army of Israel twenty miles east to Shiloh and destroyed its shrine. Another clue to the fate of Shiloh appears in Ps 78:59–64:

> God has heard and has become angry, he has completely rejected Israel.
>
> He abandoned the tent of Shiloh, a tent he inhabited among humanity.
>
> He gave over his might to captivity, and his splendor in the hand of an enemy.

He handed his people over to the sword and he became angry
against his heritage.

Fire devoured his young men, and his virgins made no cry of
distress.

His priests fell by the sword and his widows did not weep.

The psalmist seems to know the traditions that appear in 1 Sam
4. Yet it too says little about the actual status of Shiloh after God
abandoned the tent there. In the language of the ancient Near East,
when a deity is said to abandon a place, it is often an indication
that the site was overrun by an enemy of the deity's people.[5] Psalm
78 could certainly be read as an expression of military defeat construed as divine abandonment. Even so, the exact fate of Shiloh is
clouded in obscurity in this biblical text.

When we turn to archaeological data, however, things become
clearer. Shiloh has been identified with the modern site of Khirbet
Seilun. Multiple excavation teams have confirmed a destruction
level that can be dated to the middle of the eleventh century BCE.[6]
This destruction was most likely the work of the Philistines and
its date corresponds to the period in which the story of the loss of
the ark is set. There is also strong evidence that the destroyed city
included a temple complex. Indeed, the Bible intimates as much
in a few places where the word *hekal*, meaning "temple," is used
to describe the shrine at Shiloh rather than the word for "tent" (1
Sam 1:9; 3:3).[7]

We may conclude, therefore, from the convergence of the
biblical evidence with archaeological data that Shiloh was once a
worship center for early Israel and that it was destroyed after the
battle near Aphek in the middle of the eleventh century.[8] If the

---

5. This ancient concept can be traced all the way back to Sumerian culture
in Mesopotamia. See Fleming, "Ur," 8.

6. Finkelstein, Bunimovitz, and Lederman, *Shiloh*, 389.

7. Some Septuagint manuscripts attest the word "house," another common term for "temple" in Hebrew.

8. Donald Schley has argued that Jeremiah refers to the destruction
wrought by the Assyrians when they invaded the northern kingdom in the
eighth century rather than the events recounted in 1 Sam 4. See Schley, *Shiloh*.

Bible's reticence on the topic of Shiloh and its shrine is any indication, it seems likely that their destruction was a tragic event that few wanted to remember.

Jeremiah is the only prophet to mention Shiloh, and he does so more than once (see 26:6–9). As we noted above, he instructed the people to go to Shiloh but did not explain why. The most plausible reason for Jeremiah's directive was to remind the people of Jerusalem that God had already allowed his worship center to be captured and destroyed once before. This in turn suggests that Jeremiah's contemporaries knew the story of Shiloh's destruction in the days of Eli. Perhaps the ruins of the temple complex were still visible in the sixth century BCE.

Jeremiah was thus reminding his audience of their collective past. And like Hosea, Jeremiah reminded the people of a tragic past, a time when they fell away from following Yahweh and disaster ensued. He called them to evaluate their confidence in the Jerusalem temple in light of the story of Shiloh. Using the precedent of Shiloh, Jeremiah argued that if Yahweh let Israel's first permanent worship center be destroyed, then Jerusalem too might be at risk.

Jeremiah, like Hosea, functioned as a historian for Israel, exhibiting a willingness to be transparent about Israel's past. Moreover, there is an added twist to this sermon on Jerusalem and Shiloh. It is likely that Jeremiah himself was a descendant of the house of Eli.[9] Jeremiah's hometown was Anathoth, the city to which Abiathar the priest was banished by Solomon (1 Kgs 2:26–27) after the failed coup led by Adonijah in the wake of David's death (1 Kgs 1:5–10). Abiathar's expulsion was said to fulfill the word of Yahweh that was spoken against the house of Eli in Shiloh (1 Kgs 2:27). Combining these data suggests that Jeremiah was reminding his audience in the Jerusalem Temple of a tragedy to be ascribed to the failings of his own family. So the level of transparency is

---

Yet the prophet's reference to Shiloh as a central cult site suggests a time when Shiloh functioned the same way Jerusalem did in Jeremiah's day. That Shiloh is mentioned twice in Jeremiah (chapters 7 and 26) and once in Ps 78:60 suggests that it became a kind of shorthand that summarized the events of 1 Sam 4.

9. Lundbom, *Jeremiah 1–20*, 107.

even greater than one might recognize at first glance. Jeremiah was willing to recall the uncomfortable past that all of Israel shared. Yet he was also willing to tell the specific story of the failed leadership of Eli and his sons, a story of his own family.

As I have argued elsewhere, this attitude toward the past extends beyond the prophets Hosea and Jeremiah.[10] The biblical writers have a relentless drive to be honest about the past as exhibited in their willingness to expose the failings of people who are otherwise depicted as persons approved by God. Hosea and Jeremiah provide clear examples of the theme of historical transparency, which is an important component of the Old Testament prophetic tradition.

CORNEL WEST

Cornel West (b. 1953), Professor of the Practice of Public Philosophy at Harvard Divinity School, is an indefatigable writer, lecturer, and activist. West has taught multiple generations of university students and, via his lecture circuit, touched the lives of hundreds of thousands across North America. Prior to his appointment at Harvard, West taught at Union Theological Seminary and Princeton University. He has criss-crossed the US several times each year, speaking at universities, churches, prisons, and other venues for many civic organizations. His influence extends to his numerous essays, articles, and books. Academically gifted at an early age, West was among the first wave of affirmative action college students who entered Harvard College. He finished his degree in Near Eastern languages and civilizations in just three years, graduating in 1973, and received a Ph.D. in philosophy from Princeton in 1980. While his work has centered on matters of race in America, the range of West's scholarship is broad, addressing ethics and Marxism as well as various facets of Christian theology. He speaks in the academy but also in the street, working with poets, rap artists, and

10. See Bembry, "Cornel West."

TV talk show hosts like Tavis Smiley to bring a social critique to bear on the American context.

West assesses the ways of the world today from a radical democratic viewpoint. He is a Christian but he is suspicious of the way Christians—both conservative and liberal—use religion to prop up the status quo. He is attracted to the love of Jesus illustrated at the crucifixion and to the way in which Jesus loves his way through the darkness and the vale of tears that characterizes life for so many people in the world. West is also an outspoken critic of the excess of American materialism and what he calls the commodification of almost everything in American life. Values such as love and compassion become hard to find in a world where everything seems to be for sale. In his writing and teaching Cornel West tries to live out the Old Testament prophetic tradition of speaking the truth that many often do not want to hear. In particular, West stands in the tradition of Frederick Douglass, Ella Baker, Fannie Lou Hamer, and W. E. B. Du Bois, seeking to tell the vicious story of slavery in America, of the Jim Crow system that followed it, and of how the legacy of those institutions continues to affect people today.

Through his many writings and speeches, West has called the people of the US to deepen their level of introspection, to adopt a self-critical stance, and to practice historical transparency. West's awareness of history in all its beauty and ugliness serves as a powerful example of the call to transparency, which makes it a fitting counterpart to the biblical perspectives espoused by Hosea and Jeremiah.

America has long been a place where the quest for truthful history has been viewed by many with ambivalence at best and downright antagonism at worst. West argues that "No other democratic nation revels in self-deception in regard to its history as we do in the US."[11] He also notes that Americans are particularly fascinated with the future and desire to talk about it as if the past did not exist.[12] Americans by and large are locked into a state of

---

11. West, *Democracy Matters*, 41.

12. West, interview with Christopher Lydon. West says elsewhere that the

what he calls "historical amnesia."[13] West, of course, is not alone in this observation. The Frenchman Alexis de Tocqueville noted a similar orientation among Americans when he visited the US in the 1830s. Discussing democratic ideals in general and America in particular, de Tocqueville wrote:

> The woof of time is every instant broken, and the track of generations effaced. Those who went before are soon forgotten; of those who will come after, no one has any idea: the interest of man is confined to those in close propinquity to himself. . . . Not only does democracy make every man forget his ancestors, but it hides his descendants and separates his contemporaries from him; it throws him back forever upon himself alone, and threatens in the end to confine him entirely within the solitude of his own heart.[14]

Downplaying the importance of our past is a part of the American psyche that serves existential and collective purposes. Indeed, it is an essential part of the American immigrant dream: for all the people who have come to America to escape an oppressive past, America constituted a new start, offering individuals a way to transcend their own history and the history of their families. America is celebrated as a place where people can make a new future for themselves, a life supposedly free of the burdens of history.

The American ambivalence toward history, which leans strongly in the direction of an outright suspicion of history, has also infiltrated American Christianity, as can be seen in much of the rhetoric that issued from nineteenth-century Christian pulpits. The shift away from classically educated and university-trained clergy to preachers who put their trust in people's common sense went hand in hand with the impulse to see in history the

---

US is a forward-looking nation rather than a backward-looking one, and thus possesses a limited sense of history. See West, *Prophetic Thought*, 23.

13. West, *Prophetic Reflections*, 104. In this book West notes that one of the most disappointing features in our moment in history is the lack of a historical sense (148).

14. Tocqueville, *Democracy in America*, 120–21.

tradition-laden, heavy hand of the past.[15] The founding leaders of a number of Christian groups, such as Elias Smith, Lorenzo Dow, Alexander Campbell, Barton Stone, Joseph Smith, and William Miller, viewed history as a great record of apostasy, and thus saw history as something to be transcended in order to return to the primitive Christian order of things.[16] This dismissive outlook on history was shared by many political thinkers as well. Democratic and individualistic perspectives undermined a reverence for the past.[17] The unintended result of this outlook is a blindness to the failures of the past, those times when Americans have not lived up to their own collective ideals.

American culture will, on occasion, revel in uncovering the foibles of a politician or a certain celebrity. The American penchant for exposé is often driven by the desire for titillation or a collective *Schadenfreude*. But America lacks the collective desire to plumb the depths of what Cornel West calls "the nightside of our existence": racism, patriarchal and classist restrictions on the right to vote, the wanton seizure of native lands, and national haughtiness, jingoism, and xenophobia, to name but a few.[18] West often speaks and writes of the importance of a self-critical stance.[19] And he insists that in order to cultivate that stance America must adopt a historicist sensibility—a willingness to read history seriously and voraciously.[20]

West attributes this lamentable situation in part to the crisis of the widespread accommodation of American religion to the political and cultural status quo.[21] There is far too little willingness among people of faith to cut against the cultural grain in order to unmask this clandestine "nightside." West speaks of inserting into this fragile democratic experiment called America a "blue

15. Hatch, *Democratization of American Christianity*, 162.

16. Ibid., 166–68.

17. Appleby, "Intellectual Underpinnings," 15.

18. West, "Introduction," xviii.

19. West, *Prophetic Thought*, 143.

20. Ibid., 144.

21. West, *Prophetic Fragments*, ix.

note"—a note of dissonance in the form of an honest, critical assessment of American culture that begins with telling the truth about the US—not only about individual citizens but also about our collective past.[22] This prophetic call for historical awareness moves beyond the melodramatic and merely practical notion of "remembering the past so as not to repeat its mistakes." Of course, George Santayana's advice has value. Yet, for West, knowing one's historical nightside has a far richer, far more profound function. It keeps all people grounded in the awareness of the human, indeed all too human, temptation to lash out at others in a self-serving manner in order to protect systems that ensure the status quo, propping them up with self-indulgent narratives. The past reminds people of what they are capable of becoming, and it helps everyone understand the way things are in the present. The inclination to evade this history leads to a very one-sided retelling of the past, a triumphant symphony with no minor chords.

West provides many examples of this introspective and transparent perspective in his work. He goes beyond the romanticized and homogenous past and, using a Marxist lens, probes the intricacies of history's sinister side.[23] West also applies this transparency to the story of African American struggle in the US. He brings a deep awareness of how the vicious legacy of slavery and Jim Crow segregation continues to have devastating effects on all facets of life in America.

CONCLUSION

West's call for people to take stock of their past, on both the individual and societal level, is reminiscent of the words of Hosea and Jeremiah. Like these biblical prophets, West embodies a courageous willingness to tell the truth about America's past—especially those moments many would prefer to forget. These lessons from the nightside of American history serve to illustrate where things

22. West, *Prophesy Deliverance*, 10.
23. West, *Prophetic Reflections*, 172.

have gone wrong, reminding all people what they are capable of. A voice that recalls what has been forgotten is not always welcome. Like Jeremiah, West has been threatened with bodily harm for speaking as he does.[24] The willingness to tell the truth about our own individual pasts and the collective past of our society is part of the legacy of the prophetic tradition. West provides us with an eloquent model of how historical openness can be practiced in twenty-first-century America.

24. West, interview with Brian Lamb.

4

Indictment of Empty Worship

"TELEVANGELISM" IS A TERM that grew out of the late twentieth-century North American context and refers to teaching Christianity through the medium of television. Perhaps the most famous televangelists were Jimmy Swaggert and Jim Bakker, whose ministries broadcast programs centered around preaching and fund-raising. Their programs were loosely modeled on the average Protestant Christian worship service, consisting of worship music, prayer, exhortation through sermons, testimonials from various people, and calls for offerings. Bakker built a theme park called Heritage USA and founded the Trinity Broadcasting Network on which his program *The PTL (Praise the Lord) Club* appeared regularly. Bakker was convicted of financial mismanagement and his media empire was dismantled. Swaggert built a syndicated television program that spanned the US during the 1970s and 80s, showcasing his preaching and singing. His association with prostitutes led to his downfall, however, and many of the media outlets for his program evaporated.

These two men and their tragic stories epitomize the worst form of empty religiosity, espousing religious convictions while living a life in contradiction to the message they professed. Bakker and Swaggert used components of worship and the appearance of piety to raise millions of dollars from those who trusted them as sincere religious leaders. One could look at the stories of these two men as illustrative of a kind of vain religiosity, an approach to faith that focuses on external trappings without regard to the integrity of living out the ethics informed by that faith. It will surely come as no surprise that empty religiosity was a problem long before the advent of televangelism. In this chapter we will look at the prophetic tradition's response to this problem and see that even in ancient Israel and Judah insincere religious expression was all too common.

The Old Testament bears ample witness to the practice of empty ritual without ethical transformation within ancient Israel. When addressing this issue, the prophetic idiom employs a critique of sacrificial offerings, insincere worship, and ritual assemblies in the face of widespread disobedience. While this sentiment appears throughout the prophets of the eighth century (Isaiah, Micah, Amos, and Hosea) and the sixth century (Jeremiah), it can also be seen in the Psalms, Proverbs, and even 1 Samuel. We begin our survey in the opening chapter of Isaiah (1:10–15):

> Hear the word of Yahweh you leaders of Sodom,
> Give ear to the law of our God you people of Gomorrah.
> "What to me is the multitude of your sacrifices?" says Yahweh.
> I have had enough of burnt offerings of rams and the fat of fed beasts.
> I do not delight in the blood of bulls or of lambs or of he-goats.
> When you come to see my face, who seeks this from your hand—a trampling of my courts?
> Stop bringing in vain offerings. Incense is an abomination to me.
> New moon and Sabbath and the calling of an assembly.
> I cannot endure iniquity and solemn assembly.
> Your new moons and your appointed feasts my soul hates, they have become a burden to me—a burden I am weary of bearing.

> When you spread forth your hands, I hide my eyes
> from you,
> Even though you make many prayers, I will not lis-
> ten, your hands are full of blood.

This scene depicts Yahweh as a God who is weary of what we might call the religious trappings of Israelite faith, identified as sacrifices, special assemblies, weekly (Sabbath) and monthly (new moon) celebrations, and prayer. In this critique we see Israel's sacrificial system in outline. The "sacrifices" (v. 11) were offerings that were shared between God, the priest, and the one making the offering.[1] Burnt offerings—animals that were slaughtered and completely burned on the altar—and the burning of incense on the altar as a fragrant offering are referred to as "vain offerings." Since some of the sacrifices were shared with the priests and the one bringing the sacrifice, humans gained something from them. The burnt offering, however, was imagined to be given completely over to God. The prophetic voice indicts all of these sacrificial practices, depicting God as weary of his people's efforts.

In a similar manner, holidays are targeted in this prophetic indictment. Festive gatherings like the new moon celebrations and appointed feasts, which probably included Passover (centered around the barley harvest in early spring), the Feast of Weeks (centered around the wheat harvest in late spring), and the Feast of Tabernacles (centered around the harvest of summer crops in the fall) are also looked upon with divine derision. Even the more somber times on the calendar such as the weekly Sabbath and the solemn assemblies are looked upon with divine disdain. These moments on the calendar might have been viewed by some as a kind of sacrifice; for example, the solemn assemblies might have called for fasting to show repentance. Similarly the Sabbath involved a loss of production or wages for some, since it constituted a weekly work stoppage. Even prayer, which in later tradition becomes something of a replacement for sacrifice following the loss of the altar in the Jerusalem Temple, is rejected by God.[2]

1. Kaiser, *Isaiah 1–12*, 29.
2. Kugel, "Topics in Spirituality of the Psalms," 129.

Later in the book of Isaiah, another prophetic voice calls the practice of fasting into question. Often seen as a pious display of repentance or lamenting grief directed at the deity, fasting became a target of critique in Jesus' day. Yet his chiding of those who make their faces sullen to accentuate the apparent suffering they undergo for God (Matt 6:16–18) are prefigured centuries earlier in the book of Isaiah (58:2–7). In this text the prophet declares, "In the day of your fast you seek your own pleasure, and oppress all your workers" (v. 3). Later the prophet, speaking for God, concludes, "Is not this the fast that I choose; to loose the bonds of wickedness, to untie the straps of the yoke, to let the oppressed ones go free and to break every yoke? Is it not to share your bread with the hungry, and to bring the homeless poor into your house; when you see the naked, to cover them and avoid hiding yourself from your own flesh?" (vv. 6–7). The critique turns on the basic principle of fasting: giving something up for a higher purpose. The prophet notes that one might choose, instead of fasting from food, to forgo profits in order to avoid exploiting working people. Or one might chose to forgo benefits from a system that is predicated on wickedness or oppression in order that everyone can experience a just and proper life. Finally, one might even choose to give one's food to poor people, or to surrender space in one's home so that homeless people can have shelter, or to hand over extra clothes to those in need.

Isaiah is not the only prophet to talk this way. Amos, another eighth-century prophet, expresses a similar sentiment in his message from God to the people. Among the many targets Amos highlights in his sermons is empty religiosity:

> I hate, I despise your feasts, I take no delight in your solemn assemblies.
> Whenever you offer up burnt offerings and your grain offerings, I am not pleased.
> I do not look upon the fellowship offering of your fatlings.
> Remove from me the noise of your songs, I will not listen to the song of your harps.

But let justice roll like the waters and proper ways
like an ever-flowing stream.
Did you bring near to me sacrifices and grain offerings in the wilderness forty years, O house of Israel?
(Amos 5:21–25)

Again, the feasts and solemn assemblies are targets of critique. As
seen above, the combination of these two types of holidays might
suggest a sort of spectrum whereby festive occasions, such as the
three major festivals that center upon harvest times, are on one
end and the solemn assemblies that were more somber in nature
are on the other. Juxtaposing them as Isaiah and Amos do might
constitute a way to say that all gatherings, joyous and somber, have
become displeasing to God. The sacrificial system is also included
in Amos's prophetic word. He targets burnt offerings, grain offerings, and fellowship offerings of fatlings. As we saw with Isaiah,
these multiple references to types of offerings might indicate the
same kind of spectrum we see with the assemblies. Burnt offerings would be considered more solemn in nature since the entire
animal was devoted to God. The other offerings were imagined to
be shared among God, the worshiper, and the priest.

Amos's indictment lacks any reference to prayer but does
mention songs. Not much is known about the hymnic tradition
in Israelite worship. While the psalms might have been a part of
the early worship experience of Israel, there is simply little indication of how singing and instrumental accompaniment were used
in the worship of Yahweh. Whatever the precise role music played
in Israel's worship, we see Amos deriding it along with the other
external trappings of religiosity. It seems that for Yahweh these
modes of worship were mere shams when decoupled from a true
commitment to living out the will of God in daily life.

The question posed by Amos at the end of this passage is quite
interesting. Amos seems to know of no sacrificial system practiced
during the forty years of wilderness wandering. An identical outlook on Israel's past is seen in God's words that Jeremiah repeats to
the people: "In the day I brought them out of the land of Egypt, I
did not speak to your fathers or command them concerning burnt

offerings and sacrifices" (Jer 7:22). Jeremiah in the sixth century knows of the same tradition from Amos's day. The rhetorical point being made by Amos and Jeremiah suggests that Yahweh had a relationship with Israel for a long time without the practice of sacrifice. Both prophets are pointing out that within the big picture of Israel's worship of God, the cultic aspects seen most clearly in the sacrificial system should not be of ultimate concern. To put those sacrifices on a higher plane than right conduct is a mistake.

A further echo of this type of prophetic indictment is seen in Micah, yet another eighth-century prophet. He was from Moresheth Gath, a town in southwest Judah, and he engaged in prophetic activity during the reign of Hezekiah. He explicitly declares that right conduct is much preferred by God over sacrifice:

> With what shall I come before Yahweh, (with what) shall I bow down to the High God? Shall I appear before him with burnt offerings, with two-year-old calves?
> Will Yahweh be pleased with a thousand rams, with ten thousand streams of oil?
> Shall I give my firstborn for my sin, the fruit of my body in place of the sin of my being?
> He has declared to you O human being what is good.
> What does Yahweh seek from you—except to enact justice and the love of mercy and to walk with your God humbly. (Mic 6:6–8)

Micah's words are not quite as harsh as those of Isaiah and Amos. Rather than declaring that God hates or has had enough of these offerings, Micah simply says that these things are not what pleases God. Despite the less strident tone, the point is generally the same. As he lists increasingly valuable offerings, ranging from calves to children, Micah demonstrates that Yahweh takes more delight in proper living more than in the most ostentatious offering humans can imagine.

Yet another eighth-century prophet, Hosea, spoke a word of critique against the practice of sacrifice. The prophet addressed the people on behalf of God saying, "I desire mercy (or loving kindness) rather than sacrifice, an acknowledgment of God rather than burnt offerings" (Hos 6:6). These words echo the sentiments expressed by Amos regarding the relative importance of correct behavior over against the practice of offering animals to God. The Hebrew word *ḥesed*, translated "mercy" or "loving kindness," offers some interesting nuances. Since it is in poetic parallel with "knowledge" or "acknowledgment of God," some commentators assume the word here means "kindness in moral behavior."[3] This meaning underlines the contrast Hosea drew between right conduct and the practice of sacrifice. As we will see later, Hosea was critical of the sacrificial system elsewhere in his writings (5:6–7; 8:11), depicting God preferring decency over offering sacrifices.

Those familiar with the Gospel of Matthew will recognize this quote from Hosea. Jesus recited this verse to the Pharisees when they questioned his practice of engaging in table fellowship with tax collectors and sinners (Matt 9:13), and again when they chastised him and his disciples for picking grain pods on the Sabbath (Matt 12:7). In the introduction to this book we noted Jesus' awareness of the prophetic tradition when he told his disciples they would be treated like the prophets of old. His quotation of Hosea's words reveals a further thematic connection to the Old Testament prophetic tradition.

To illustrate how this prophetic indictment of the sacrificial system extends beyond the corpus referred to as "the prophets," we turn to a story in 1 Sam 15. Saul led the armies of Israel against the Amalekites and returned victorious. Saul was under orders from the prophet Samuel to destroy the Amalekites completely—the people, their king, and all their animals. Saul had killed the people but he spared King Agag, along with all the livestock that was captured. When Samuel learned of this, he confronted Saul. The king replied that he kept the animals so that he could make an offering to Yahweh. Samuel replied, "Is Yahweh's greater delight with burnt offerings and sacrifices or obedience to Yahweh's voice? Listening (to God) is better than sacrifice, paying attention (to God) is better than the fat of rams" (1 Sam 15:22). As we saw with Micah, no explicit condemnation of the sacrificial system is given here by

3. MacIntosh, *Hosea*, 234.

Samuel. Yet following God's command is valued more than offering animals on altars.

Related to these indictments of the sacrificial system are the words of critique directed against the priests who oversaw it. I noted above the words of Hosea regarding God's desire for mercy or loving kindness rather than sacrifice (Hos 6:6). In Hosea 4–5 we see the prophet exposing the priesthood's conflict of interest. Yahweh says, "With you O priest is my contention" (Hos 4:4).[4] He continues, "Because you have rejected the knowledge, I reject you from serving as priest for me" (4:6) and adds that "They (the priests) feed on the sin of my people" (4:8). In this last verse there is likely a play on the word translated as "sin." In Hebrew the word for "sin" is the same as the word for "sin offering." These sin offerings were apparently animals that were offered to God but also were shared with the officiating priests at the altar. Hosea is drawing attention to a potential conflict of interest for priests in the sacrificial system. The more the people sinned, the more sin offerings they needed to bring. And the more sin offerings were brought, the more meat and grain the priests received.[5]

Earlier it was noted that the prophet Jeremiah shared with Amos a perspective on the history of sacrifice. He also echoes the broader divine assessment of sacrifice when he transmits a warning from God:

> Hear, O earth. I am about to bring evil upon this people,
> the fruit of their plans, because they have not listened
> to my words and they have rejected my law. What is

4. The Hebrew of this verse is a bit garbled. While the word "priest" is clear, the precise meaning of the remaining words in the above translation have been derived from the context and the suggestions by the editors of the standard critical edition of the Hebrew Bible.

5. Such a nuanced critique of priestly officiation at the sacrificial altars has led some to suggest that Hosea was a former priest. That the critique could have come from an insider who possessed an intimate understanding of the inner workings of the system would not be surprising. Although he does not make an explicit claim that Hosea was a former priest, much of Hans Walter Wolff's commentary operates with such an idea in mind. See Wolff, *Hosea*. I am not alone in this point of view of Wolff. See also Blenkinsopp, *History of Prophecy*, 85.

frankincense from Sheba to me? Or cane from a distant
land? Your burnt offerings are not acceptable, your sacrifices are not pleasing to me. (Jer 6:19–21)

As is often the case in prophetic discourse, sacrifices and burnt
offerings are juxtaposed with obedience. Although he does not attack the larger cultic system of sacrifice, Jeremiah again points out
that obedience is preferable to God when compared with sacrifice.

While the theme of cultic critique—criticism of worship acts
—is clearly pervasive in the prophetic texts of the Old Testament,
this same idea is expressed in other genres as well. In Ps 51, the
great penitential psalm attributed to David after his adulterous
affair with Bathsheba, we read the words, "For you (God) have
no delight in sacrifice. Even if I were to give a burnt offering, you
would not be pleased. The sacrifice God wants is a broken spirit,
a broken and contrite heart, O God, you will not despise" (v. 17).

Likewise, even in the book of Proverbs (21:3) we read that "to
do righteousness and justice is more acceptable to the Lord than
sacrifice." The word-pair "righteousness" and "justice," indicating
proper ways of living, will be the subject of chapter 7. Here the
terms are used to echo the sentiment of the other texts we have
examined in this chapter. Thus, even the psalms and the wisdom
tradition attest the theme of divine preference for right behavior
over cultic sacrifice.

THE POINT OF THE PROPHETIC CRITIQUE OF WORSHIP

Before considering modern-day parallels to these prophetic indictments, it is important to clarify exactly what is being addressed
by these prophets and other writers. On the one hand, some might
suggest that some of these prophets are calling for an end to cultic
rituals—the festivals, solemn assemblies, the sacrificial system,
worship songs, and prayer.[6] On the other hand, some will suggest
that these lines from the prophets are a part of a rhetorical strategy

---

6. Miranda, *Marx and the Bible*, 56–58. For Miranda (55) this prophetic
stance is foundational for showing how the God of the Bible is different from
all the other gods.

of hyperbole designed not to rid the land of these practices but rather to bring behavior into line with the mode of being expressed by all these sacrificial activities. I stand somewhere between these two extremes. I affirm the importance of avoiding the supercessionist trap that seeks to Christianize the Old Testament so that every verse points to the wholesale rejection of anything connected to later Judaism. There is a long legacy, especially among Protestant Christians, that seeks to pit all things prophetic against all things priestly in the Old Testament. The most facile reduction of this position equates all priestly activity with the Phariseeism of Jesus' day, and all things prophetic with the teachings of Jesus. Additionally, Protestants are sometimes guilty of assuming that a modern rejection of Roman Catholic priestly-oriented traditions mirrors Jesus' critique of Phariseeism, and by extension modern Judaism. Further reductions see sacrifice and the Temple as a distortion of true worship, to be juxtaposed against an elevated spirituality seen in Jesus' teachings.[7] I do not believe that these prophetic voices are calling for a full cessation of all of these outward practices that scholars label "cultic." Yet I also do not believe that these prophetic words are mere rhetorical flourishes designed to motivate persons to practice consistent integrity. The point of it all may simply be to say something like, "God is willing to grant that humans need to have outward religious or ritual manifestations of action that can provide substance for a commitment to following God. Even so, humans should not assume that those outward religious or ritual manifestations constitute or fully exhaust the things of preeminent importance to the deity."

CONNECTING ANCIENT CONCERNS TO TODAY

In order to identify modern-day parallels to the kind of prophetic message we have examined in this chapter, we must first determine what modern phenomena might mirror the ritual trappings that

7. The most nuanced critique of the Christian appropriation of the prophetic voice leveled against the Temple and the cult is Levenson, "Temple and the World"; see especially p. 282.

the biblical prophets derided in their day. So we must ask what aspects of contemporary Christian worship can be construed as analogous to sacrifice, solemn and festive assembly, Sabbath observance, songs, and prayer. The latter two are rather easy to deal with since the corporate practice of singing and prayer is retained today in the worship experience of many Christians. Observance of the Sabbath and participation in assemblies, both festive and solemn, might properly be construed under corporate worship on Sunday. The parallels are by no means perfect, since the Israelite notion of the Sabbath does not perfectly correspond to Christian outlooks on Sunday. Likewise, modern Christian worship is not generally centered around agricultural harvests or times of lament and repentance as was the case in ancient Israel. To be sure, some Christians follow a liturgical calendar (observing the seasons of Advent and Lent, for example) that might constitute a close parallel to ancient Israelite customs. If we think of these yearly practices in broader terms, however, the distinctions that exist blur and the similarities are indeed closely proximate.

Identifying a modern analogy for biblical sacrifice constitutes the greatest challenge on this list. Christian ritual practice does not include slaughtering animals and burning them on an altar. If we think of sacrifice more abstractly as surrendering something of value to honor God, it is easier to think of modern parallels. Giving time or money to support a church or Christian community comes to mind. The modern practice of tithing or donating 10 percent of one's income to the church is a well-defined custom that can be seen as an abstract form of sacrifice.

Thus, a search for modern-day parallels to the religious trappings that come under prophetic indictment yields practices such as prayer, singing or playing songs, Sunday church attendance, celebrations on the liturgical calendar, and giving time or money in the form of offerings (tithes).

Hosea's critique of the potential conflict of interest among priests has modern-day parallels as well. We began the chapter with two tragic examples of ministers who exploited their flocks by misappropriating the donations they received. These are by no means isolated incidents. It is axiomatic that in any realm where money is exchanged, those who work within the system face a perennial challenge to maintain integrity so that no undue benefit comes to them or their loved ones.

WILL CAMPBELL

Now that we have a sense of how the ancient indictment of empty religiosity can apply to people of faith today, we turn to modern voices who have continued this prophetic critique for Christians today—Will Campbell and César Chávez. Will Campbell spent most of his life calling Christians to avoid the outward religious trappings that so easily become a primary concern in Christian communities. Despite being raised in the Southern Baptist tradition, Campbell was never quite at home in traditional pastoral ministry centered on elaborate, ornate church buildings with corporate-style budgets and organizational structures.

Campbell's vision of the modern church is deeply rooted in a desire to recapture the simple ways of Jesus and his disciples as revealed in the New Testament. Church for Campbell is not the physical bricks-and-mortar structure that often consumes the largest portion of a church budget. Church is simply the community of confessing people—a community that exists apart from any edifice.

Campbell's perspective, which differs sharply from the way many Christians understand "church," aligns his work with the prophetic indictment of empty ritual trappings I noted above. The modern equivalent of participating in a solemn or festive assembly is going to church on Sunday or attending special worship services at certain times of the year, such as Christmas or Easter. Many Christians would assume that church attendance would involve assembling at a building to engage in acts of worship, where songs and prayer are offered up along with the presentation of tithes and offerings. Campbell often questioned the need for a building—especially an expensive building. Campbell best summed up this view in a sermon he gave at the Riverside Baptist Church on May

17, 1984, where he had been invited to speak on the issues of race and racism in America. Yet as Campbell was often wont to do, he demonstrated the deeper aspects of these problems and their relationship to poverty in the US. So he chided the wealthy Riverside Church that day with this question:

> The question we are *really* asking is "What can we do about race and racism in American culture and keep all this [gesturing to the grandeur of Riverside's sanctuary]?" and the answer, my brothers and sisters, is "nothing."[8]

Campbell goes on to point out just how difficult it would be for Riverside or even his own family to part with valuable real estate. So he is aware of the tension. Yet his deeper conviction about the futility of Christian communities tying up money in expensive property overlaps with the prophetic critique we examined above. When Christians understand their Christian identity primarily through their membership in a given Christian community that owns a beautiful building for weekly assemblies, outward ritual trappings are encroaching upon what it means to be a Christian. Related to this skewed outlook is the matter of money. If tithes and offerings are primarily being used to maintain or acquire nice buildings, one must be aware how this reality can become all-consuming and, in fact, become an end in itself. When budgets are large and building projects must be maintained, churches can often lose perspective concerning their true mission. A fascination with beautiful buildings can become one of those religious trappings that lures Christians away from what is truly important—the central message of living a life in line with what God wants.

Akin to the problem of expensive buildings is church music. I often ask students who serve on ministry staffs how much their church spends on music, and even they are often alarmed to find out just how big a line item it is on their church's budget. Music is considered by many Christians to be one of the most important areas of modern Christian worship. People choose to attend services at a church for many reasons, but their experience with the

8. Letcher, *God's Will.*

music on Sunday is often a significant factor. The flourishing of different styles of worship music has become a divisive issue in many American churches, and it is quite common now to hear of churches having separate "traditional" and "contemporary" services to appease, in part, various musical tastes. When musical styles become a deciding factor in choosing a church or an increasing percentage of a church's budget is spent on musicians and sound systems, church music risks becoming a trapping of religiosity. Like the architecture and decoration of church buildings, elaborate musical performances can detract from a church's true mission. One can, for example, imagine a church that has an aesthetically pleasing building and aesthetically pleasing music but lacks any other indication of a viable Christian community. What should one conclude about a church like this? Can it truly be called a church, in Will Campbell's sense? Walking in the prophetic tradition demands that these questions be addressed.

Another aspect of church life that may easily become an end in itself is fundraising. I argued above that the closest modern parallel to the Israelite sacrificial system is the giving of tithes and offerings in churches. The question that Will Campbell raises regarding this issue is, "How is the institutional church different from an average business or country club"? Are ministers and staff analogous to retail employees or wait staff at the country club buffet? When the success of a church is measured by the amount of weekly contributions or by its ability to attract new members who are likely to become generous donors (for example, doctors, lawyers, or financially successful entrepreneurs and business owners), one must ask how the biblical prophets and the early Christian witnesses would respond. In light of Hosea's critique of the priestly conflict of interest, one must also ask whether ministers and staff benefit disproportionately from tithes and offerings or other benefits attached to leading a prosperous community. Concerns such as these are what Will Campbell had in mind when he suggested that the American church in the main demonstrates a reality that would be totally foreign to Jesus and the first-century CE disciples.

CÉSAR CHÁVEZ

Will Campbell's sentiments were shared by César Chávez. While Chávez remained loyal to the teachings of the church in his quest for better working conditions for farm laborers, he was not unwilling to reprimand church authorities when he felt it necessary. In March 1968, in the middle of a twenty-five-day "spiritual fast," he addressed a meeting centered on Mexican-Americans and the church at the Second Annual Mexican Conference in Sacramento. In his address Chávez referred to the church as "an organization with tremendous wealth," and he asked why local parish priests did nothing to help the striking grape-farm laborers. He noted that when the strike began in Delano, none of the local priests there would help them. They even refused to allow workers seeking to hold organizational meetings to gather in church buildings —buildings that these workers had helped build through their contributions. At the end of his address Chávez expressed his idea of the church's role in the community:

> In a nutshell, what do we want the Church to do? We don't ask for more cathedrals. We don't ask for bigger churches or fine gifts. We ask for its presence with us, beside us, as Christ among us. We ask the Church to sacrifice with the people for social change, for justice, and for love of brother. We don't ask for words, we ask for deeds. We don't ask for paternalism. We ask for servanthood.[9]

Paralleling the words of Will Campbell at the Riverside Church in New York City, Chávez questions the need for opulent buildings and calls the church to allocate money to people—people the church is obligated to care for. He alludes to the notion of sacrifice as well, arguably inviting church leaders to relinquish their ties with the wealthy in deference to the "least of these," the phrase Jesus used to denote those in need.

---

9. Chávez, *Gospel of César Chávez*, 90.

CONCLUSION

Televangelism and other attempts to use elements of worship experience to raise money to line the pockets of manipulative frauds are modern manifestations of empty religiosity. Although it is enticing to assume that only high-profile mass-media charlatans are guilty of such behavior, the truth is that empty religiosity can seduce anyone. We all must be on guard against letting our faith become another mechanism to get what we want. The prophetic voices of Samuel, Isaiah, Hosea, Micah, and Jeremiah must be heard today, and people who claim to follow God and believe the words of the Bible must take heed of these vital warnings. Expressions of worship must be congruous with the way people of faith live their lives. Placing great value on outward religious actions while ignoring biblical directives for living is clearly displeasing to God, as the prophetic voices warn. The admonishments from Campbell and Chávez continue the prophetic tradition that seeks to help the people of God properly align their worship lives with their day-to-day lives avoiding the potential pitfalls of empty religiosity.

5

Concern for the Poor

WHEN I WAS A doctoral student in the late 1990s, my wife and I lived in a section of Beverly, Massachusetts, called Gloucester Crossing. Our apartment was surrounded by Section 8 triple-deckers—three-story apartments with government-subsidized rent. The people on our street could have been straight out of a Melville novel, given to screaming drunken obscenities at neighbors and passersby from a third-floor window. The lights in the small city park across the street from our apartment were repeatedly broken by those who liked to use the space for illegal drug activity and other dangerous liaisons. It was not uncommon to come home to find local law enforcement—sometimes armed with shotguns and bulletproof vests—serving a warrant on the street.

The youth of Gloucester Crossing, however, were the most interesting characters. In the park across the street it was common to see some of the preschool-age boys pulling their pants down and urinating wherever they found it convenient. Most of the kids used the F-word as mere filler in their everyday conversation, and the teenagers on our street would smoke pot and burn old couches and boat hulls in the empty lot beside our apartment for fun. Much of this was a bit of a shock to me, having grown up in a rather sheltered, conservative, middle-class, small Southern town. So it was easy for me in my narrowness to look down my nose at what I thought was the lowbrow behavior of the youngsters, incredulous that parents would tolerate such things.

It was during that period that I read Frank McCourt's best-selling memoir *Angela's Ashes*. I was taken with this gripping story of two brothers, Frankie and Malachi, who struggled along amidst deep poverty in Ireland and all sorts of family woes. Destitute, the mother of the boys sought help from the local Christian relief program. There she found dismissive, judgmental faces who believed that the poor were to blame for their plight. As I read about how the church-sponsored relief agency humiliated this desperate woman, I again looked down my nose—this time, at the supposed Christians who displayed such callous antipathy toward a family in need. But then something put a question in my head: What if Frankie and Malachi McCourt are the kids from Gloucester Crossing? I began to recognize that I looked a lot like the uncaring Christians in McCourt's novel, and I knew then that I needed to make some changes. Prior to that moment it had been easy to distance myself from poor people by seeing them as products of their own mismanagement, an ideological position shared by many in the US. This outlook is deeply rooted in American views of the rugged individual who pulls himself (yes, the cultural mythos has historically assumed this hero to be male) "up by his own bootstraps" to make his way in the world, avoiding poverty and securing financial success. Within the context of this cultural ideological backdrop, it was easy to blame poor people for their plight. But *Angela's Ashes* pried open my eyes to that kind of apathy and I began to see those kids in the park and their families in a different light.

While many churches talk about helping the poor, such talk does not always translate into substantive action. The reasons behind this are numerous and varied. As Cornel West notes,

> American religious life—notwithstanding its vast philanthropic networks and impressive charitable record—lacks a substantive social consciousness. This is so because, like so much of American life, it suffers from social amnesia. American religious people have little

memory of or sense for collective struggle and communal combat. At the level of family and individuals, this
memory and sense lingers. But at the level of larger social
groups and institutions, this memory and sense of struggle evaporates. This social amnesia prevents systemic
social analysis of power, wealth, and influence in society
from taking hold among most religious Americans. Instead, the tendency is to fall back on personalistic and
individualistic explanations for poverty, occupational
mobility, or social catastrophe.[1]

There is a certain irony in the fact that many Christians, myself
included, struggle to empathize with poor people, given Jesus'
commitment to the poor and outcast of his day. In this chapter we
will examine a number of prophets who in many ways prefigured
the kind of stance Jesus takes on this issue. We will connect the
prophetic tradition's theme of concern for the poor with modern
voices who demonstrate the same compassion.

The Old Testament prophets provide a veritable chorus of
calls for aid to poor people. Before examining a number of individual texts, it will be helpful to review the Hebrew words that are
used to denote poor people and the connection they have with
the notion of being oppressed. Doing so will allow us to construct
a clearer picture of just who these people were in the context of
ancient Israel.

One of the words used to demarcate poor people in the Hebrew Bible is *'ebyon* and it appears often in the prophetic books
(Isa 14:30; 25:4; 29:19; 32:6–7; 41:7; Ezek 16:49; 18:12; 22:29;
Amos 2:6; 4:1; 5:12; 8:4; 8:6; Jer 2:34; 5:28; 20:13; 22:16). The law in
Exodus protects the *'ebyon* from perversion of justice (Exod 23:6),
a theme that will also appear in Amos and Ezekiel, as we will see
below. The Deuteronomic law enjoins the wealthy to lend to the
'ebyon whatever is sufficient for their needs (Deut 15:3–11). According to the book of Proverbs, those who show kindness to the
'ebyon will receive kindness from Yahweh (Prov 19:17) and will be
blessed (Prov 22:9).

---

1. West, *Prophetic Fragments*, x.

Another word used to refer to the poor is *dal*, which frequently appears in poetic parallel with *'ebyon* in the Hebrew Bible (1 Sam 2:8; Job 5:16; Ps 72:13; 82:4; 113:7; Prov 14:31; Isa 14:30; 25:4; Amos 4:1; 8:6). Words that are paired in parallel structures are often synonymous, allowing the biblical writer to emphasize a single point by using two expressions, as in Ps 113:7: "He [God] raises up the poor (*dal*) from the dust, and lifts the needy (*'ebyon*) from the ash heap." The word *dal* appears a number of times in the prophetic books too (Isa 10:2; 11:4; 14:30; 25:4; 26:6; Jer 4:4–5; 39:10; Amos 2:7; 4:1; 5:11; 8:6; Zeph 3:12). As we saw with *'ebyon*, the law protects the *dal* from legal prejudice; in one passage, *dal* is juxtaposed with "the great," depicting the *dal* as small and powerless, lacking the communal respect afforded to "the great" (Lev 19:15). In the book of Proverbs the *dal* are described as those whose possessions are withheld from them (14:31; 22:16; 28:8) or even stolen from them (22:22), suggesting victimization.

A third Hebrew word used by the biblical prophets to denote poor people who are oppressed by more powerful elements of society is ' *ani*. Like *dal* and *'ebyon*, ' *ani* describes persons who have experienced economic hardship and are protected by law (Lev 19:10; 23:22). Deuteronomic law enjoins the people to "open their hands to the ' *ani*" (Deut 15:11). The book of Proverbs depicts them as potential victims of legal manipulation (Prov 22:22–23; 31:9), and those who give them aid are upheld as exemplars (Prov 31:20). In the prophetic corpus *dal* may refer to victims of oppression (Isa 3:14–15; 10:2; 32:7; Ezek 16:49; 18:12; 22:29; Amos 8:4; Hab 3:14), victims who find refuge in God (Isa 14:32; 41:17; Zeph 3:12), or persons whom Israel is commanded to protect (Isa 58:7). Sometimes Israel's treatment of the *dal* is cited as an indicator of how effectively the nation is dispensing justice and practicing fairness (Jer 22:16).

This brief overview of Hebrew terms for the poor helps to clarify the range of meanings these words convey. While "poor," "needy," and "afflicted" indicate economic hardship, these words also convey a sense of legal and social vulnerability, an important consideration to bear in mind as we turn to the words of the prophets.

The eighth-century prophet Amos champions the needs of the poor quite often and uses all three of the Hebrew words noted above in his discourse. In his prophecies against the nations he addresses Israel and says,

> Thus says Yahweh,
> For three transgressions of Israel and for four, I will not revoke the punishment.
> Because they sell the righteous for silver and the needy (*'ebyon*) for a pair of shoes,
> they trample the head of the poor (*dal*) into the dust of the earth,
> and turn aside the way of the afflicted (*'ani*) (Amos 2:6–7).

Righteous people and the poor are being objectified and treated like a commodity that one can buy and sell. This treatment dehumanizes people in need, and Amos depicts this behavior as unacceptable and worthy of divine censure.

In another passage the prophet rebukes the women of Bashan, a northern pastureland, and Samaria, the capital city of the northern kingdom, Israel. Amos says,

> Hear this word you heifers of Bashan, who are on the mountain of Samaria,
> who oppress the poor (*dal*), who smash the needy (*'ebyon*). (Amos 4:1)

Commentators agree that Amos is targeting a group of wealthy people—here, specifically women—who are enjoying the extravagant wealth that accrued to Israel in the days of Jeroboam II and were apathetic toward those in greatest need among them.[2] The Bashan was (and still is) fertile pastureland in Israel, quite suitable for cattle. While "heifer" in English carries unflattering connotations, it was probably not considered to be an insult to these women in Amos's day. The image of cattle grazing in lush pastures

---

2. Mays, *Amos*, 2. See more recently, Paul, *Amos*, 2.

poignantly depicts the relative wealth of the well-fed elite juxta-posed with the hungry and needy poor.[3]

The prophet elsewhere issues a warning to those who mal-treat the poor:

> Because you trample on the poor (*dal*) and take from them a measure of grain, houses of hewn stone you have built but you shall not live in them. High-quality vineyards you have planted but you shall not drink their wine. For I know your many transgressions and the mul-titude of your sins. You are oppressors of the innocent, takers of bribes, ones who turn away the poor (*'ebyon*) at the gate. (Amos 5:11–12)

The point Amos is making in the first few lines is quite clear: God is not pleased with social apathy among the wealthy toward those who lack. The significance of the last line might not be as trans-parent, however. The notion of the poor getting turned away at the gate refers to the institutions of justice and legal protection. In Israel court cases were heard at the city's main gate in the presence of the elders, who would act as judges or adjudicators. Amos refers to those who push people away from the gate to prevent their case from being heard. This practice took advantage of the community's lack of advocacy on behalf of poor individuals, who probably had little social standing and therefore had no recourse in such a case.

On yet another occasion the prophet returns to the theme of concern for poor people. He says:

> Hear this, you who trample the needy (*'ebyon*) and bring the oppressed (*'ani*) of the land to an end, say-ing, "When will the New Moon be over that we may sell grain, and the Sabbath that we may offer wheat for sale, that we may make the ephah small and the shekel great and deal deceitfully with false balances, that we may buy the poor (*dal*) for silver and the needy (*'ebyon*) for a pair of sandals?" (Amos 8:4–6)

3. Paul, *Amos*, 128.

The needy and oppressed are depicted by Amos as being trampled, and this treatment is directly linked to the question that, no doubt, was being asked by the employers of these people: "When can we dispense with these holidays and Sabbaths that call for work stoppage?" Further, they ask, "When can we return to doing what we do—making money by cheating on the measures for the wheat (*ephah*) and currency (*shekel*) that we pay to the poor and needy, all the while treating them like a commodity?" We will have more to say about this text in the next chapter as it relates to the way working people are treated. For now our focus is on the poverty in which Amos's neighbors live. This passage echoes Amos's use of the image of selling the needy in exchange for footwear (Amos 2:6–7). The repetition might suggest that this was a stock saying in Amos's proclamations. In any case, these multiple calls for fair treatment of the poor clearly illustrate one of Amos's chief concerns.

Isaiah too indicts the leaders of Israel for maltreatment of the poor. God speaks through him saying, "It is you who have devoured the vineyard, the spoil of the poor (*'ani*) is in your houses. What is it for you when you crush my people, when you grind the face of the poor (*'ani*)?" (Isa 3:14–15).

Here the leaders are held responsible for devouring the vineyard, which is symbolic of the nation (see 1:8 and 5:1–7). This devouring is explained as the exploitation of the poor. The phrase "the spoil of the poor" likely refers to crops that should have been left in the field for the poor to glean, or it might simply point more generally to commodities that the poor needed to survive. For all of this the leaders receive divine censure.

Later Isaiah brings another indictment regarding justice for the poor:

> Woe to those who decree iniquitous decrees, and the
>   writers who keep writing oppression,
> to turn aside the needy (*dal*) from justice and to rob the
>   afflicted (*'ani*) of my people of their right,
> that widows may be their spoil and that they may make
>   the fatherless their prey" (Isa 10:1–2).

Here the prophet directs his critique at those who establish legal decrees that favor the wealthy at the expense of the poor. The widow and the orphan are linked to the poor in this context because of their tenuous status.[4] Without anyone to advocate on their behalf, they were liable to manipulation in legal contexts, and here Isaiah underlines that fact.

Like Amos and Isaiah, the prophet Jeremiah calls attention to the plight of the poor. He says,

> Like a basket full of birds, their houses are full of treachery,
> therefore they have become great and rich, they have
> grown fat and sleek.
> They know no bounds in deeds of wickedness;
> they do not judge the cause of the orphan with justice to
> make them prosper
> and they do not defend the rights of the needy (*'ebyon*)
> (Jer 5:27–28).

Once again, the context is the legal defense of the needy. As noted before, without the kind of advocacy the wealthy could count on, the needy who sought recourse from the law were vulnerable to manipulation by those with power.

Finally, we turn to the warnings of Ezekiel, the sixth-century prophet from a priestly family who experienced the initial wave of the Babylonian exile. In Ezekiel's words we see further warnings about mistreating poor people. In a list of all the ways God's people have been faithless to God's demands, after condemning those prophets who whitewash iniquity, God says, "The people of the land have practiced extortion and committed robbery. They have oppressed the poor (*'ani*) and needy (*'ebyon*)" (Ezek 22:29). Here oppression is linked with financial manipulation and theft.

It is clear that the biblical prophetic tradition speaks out on behalf of poor people and those who lack social standing. Among the prophets active from the eighth century BCE down to the days of exile in the sixth century, there is a recurrent concern for poor people victimized by legal decisions, and the prophets repeatedly condemn social apathy toward the plight of these people.

4. Kaiser, *Isaiah 1–12*, 227.

DOROTHY DAY

Of all the champions of the poor in the US in the last century, Dorothy Day must rank somewhere near the top. Her tireless efforts to address the needs of so many people in their time of need are virtually peerless. During the early part of the twentieth century, she had ample opportunity to witness the profound levels of poverty during the Great Depression of the 1930s, when so many people were out of work and in need of food, clothing, and shelter. Along with her dear friend Peter Maurin, Day worked tirelessly for the well-being of people in need. She had a lifelong friendship with Maurin, who had been involved in the Sillon Movement, a reformist Catholic organization committed to spiritual renewal that formed in response to Pope Leo XIII's 1891 encyclical calling for social justice and a more equitable distribution of material assets across class lines. Maurin exercised a formative influence on Day's thinking. Together they founded *The Catholic Worker*, a publication designed to shed light on the plight of working people. Day and Maurin also established over thirty "houses of hospitality"—their name for havens of rest for people needing something to eat, a place to spend the night, and caring people with whom to have fellowship. These houses of hospitality were more than just soup kitchens. Day believed that it was important to obscure the line between the ones serving the food and the ones receiving it so that no one was made to feel inferior in any way. Wanting to do more than helping people to meet the immediate needs of the body, Day committed to living in these houses of hospitality. This enabled her to connect with poor people on a level different from people who staffed soup kitchens and then went home to distant communities. Her lot was clearly with the poor. As one of her biographers, Robert Coles, noted, "Day and her fellow Catholic Workers are not the kind of reformers who live in one world while hoping to change another."[5] Day's perspective and her community houses of hospitality constitute an important exception to Cornel

5. Coles, *Dorothy Day*, 111.

West's analysis, cited at the beginning of this chapter, of social apathy among religious people.

Because of her deep level of commitment, Dorothy Day was able to invoke aid for the poor with a deep moral authority Her invocation to feed the hungry of the world was a constant in her work. Day lived out the biblical injunction to do more than addressing a person in need with well-wishes (Jas 2:15–16) each day of her life.

Day called the church to do more for the poor than provide charity. She said it seemed to her that "priests were more like Cain than Abel" and that the church offered "plenty of charity but too little justice."[6] In pursuit of justice for the poor, she sought to address more than the proximate causes of poverty for individual people. She also wanted Christians to appreciate the systemic causes of poverty.

Day's view of poverty had not only biblical but philosophical underpinnings. In her autobiography, *The Long Loneliness*, she quotes at length from an essay by William James that illustrates the ideals she admired in those around her.

> Among us English-speaking peoples especially do the praises of poverty need once more to be boldly sung. We have grown literally afraid to be poor. We despise anyone who elects to be poor in order to simplify and save his inner life. If he does not join the general scramble, we deem him spiritless and lacking in ambition. We have lost the power even of imagining what the ancient realization of poverty could have meant; the liberation from material attachments, the unbribed soul, the manlier indifference, the paying our way by what we are and not by what we have, the right to fling away our life at any moment irresponsibly, —the more athletic trim, in short, the moral fighting shape.[7]

This attitude toward possessions and wealth permeated Day's being and she surrounded herself with like-minded friends.

6. Day, *Long Loneliness*, 150.

7. Day, *Long Loneliness*, 119.

The preservation of human dignity was a passion for Dorothy Day especially as it related to the poor. As a young woman she signed on to work as a nurse at King's County Hospital during World War I.[8] Her first patient was a ninety-six-year-old woman who refused to let anyone bathe her until she was given her wig. When the other nurses insisted that the elderly woman let them give her a bath, Day realized that their efforts to follow hospital regulations were doing more harm than good for the patient. The nurses were insisting that the woman accept what they sought to give her, while ignoring what the woman so desperately wanted. Day sought a compromise that allowed the elderly patient to wear a cap so as to address the woman's concern about her hair loss.

Day used these experiences to shape her approach to poor people as well. She rightly understood that there was something potentially dehumanizing in giving people food and shelter as "handouts." She spoke of the profound impact Upton Sinclair's 1906 novel *The Jungle* had upon her in her early years. She could see the experiences of Jurgis Rukus, Sinclair's fictitious Lithuanian immigrant, mirrored in the lives of the men and women who came to her in need. The hospitality houses were set up so that people could volunteer alongside the workers serving the food. The servers were, after all, volunteers like Dorothy and Peter. Day credits this perspective to Maurin's insistence that aid must be given face to face rather than distributed by a faceless institution. Maurin and Day knew that hungry, impoverished people needed more than their physical needs met. They knew such people needed a sympathetic ear, a shoulder to cry on, and someone to help them live out God's call in their lives. Day had a policy of not forcing her beliefs on those who frequented the houses of hospitality. She did not require them to hear her message before they were fed. Such an approach was simply not her style. Day believed that the poor and hungry were to be fed—period. Demanding some sort of reciprocity from them violated her view of things, a perspective that was (and is) quite unique among Christian charities.

8. Day, *Long Loneliness*, 89.

Day's vision of assistance to the poor carries forth the prophetic vision from ancient Israel. Hers is a hopeful vision, one that calls everyone to make a difference for people in need. Her approach is summed up in her June 1946 column in *The Catholic Worker*:

> What we would like to do is change the world—make it a little simpler for people to feed, clothe, and shelter themselves as God intended them to do. And, by fighting for better conditions, by crying out unceasingly for the rights of the workers, of the poor, of the destitute—the rights of the worthy and the unworthy poor, in other words—we can, to a certain extent, change the world; we can work for the oasis, the little cell of joy and peace in a harried world. We can throw our pebble in the pond and be confident that its ever widening circle will reach around the world.[9]

MYLES HORTON

About the same time that Dorothy Day and Peter Maurin began publishing their paper, a young man from rural Tennessee was thinking along the same lines. Myles Horton (1905–1990) was an educator, activist, and organizer who was one of the founders of the Highlander Folk School near Monteagle, Tennessee. Horton was born and raised in the rural West Tennessee town of Savannah. His parents were educators and they raised the young Horton along with his brothers and sister in the Presbyterian Church. Horton experienced an awakening one summer during his college days at Cumberland Presbyterian College in Lebanon, Tennessee. Horton was working in a rural area of the state, trying to organize summer Vacation Bible School programs when he witnessed the more pressing needs of Depression-era life. He saw that rather than Bible lessons, people needed to know how to test their wells for typhoid and how to earn a decent wage for their work. Horton saw how the lumber industry had come in and employed local

9. Day, "Love Is the Measure."

people until they had clear-cut all the timber in the region, leaving many of the locals with the hard choice of staying near their homes but giving up their jobs or moving along to another region where the clear-cutting continued. Having a personal perspective on all these concerns in rural communities enabled Horton to see the effects of the deep poverty that ravaged Tennessee in the late 1920s. When he sought the advice of ministers whom he trusted, one of them, Abram Nightingail, suggested that he needed more education if he was going to help people address these systemic problems. So he went to study with Reinhold Niebuhr at Union Theological Seminary in New York City. From there Horton moved to Chicago, where he first learned of the Danish Folk School tradition, an educational model that encourages adults to learn from each other based on past experiences. Horton was so taken with this pedagogical concept that he moved to Denmark for a time to experience it firsthand. This paradigm constituted the foundation upon which he established Highlander a few years later. The school became the way to approach the questions he encountered during his first trip to East Tennessee as a college student. Horton's Highlander Folk School became a model for addressing needs and formulating solutions that people everywhere could implement to address their problems.

Horton's compassion for the poor people of East Tennessee helped him to see that they had been victimized by a number of entities, such as the timber industry. Although the logging companies provided jobs for some people in the area, the jobs were low-paying and short-lived. In order to continue working, the people of the region were faced with losing their jobs or leaving behind extended family and moving with the timber businesses to other parts of the country. A key natural resource of the region had been depleted and the vast majority of the timber profits were pocketed by the industry. The jobs and the natural resources were lost in one fell swoop.

Following the departure of the predatory timber companies, the federal government tried to solve the problem with federal aid programs. Although these too brought temporary relief for some, the external nature of the programs deterred many people from participating. Church organizations had sought to help East Tennessee too, and Horton himself had been a part of the YMCA's efforts in the region. Yet over the years Myles Horton saw that these efforts had flaws that alienated many local people, like the condescending assumption that the answers to problems in the region could only be achieved through external assistance.

Horton was able to succeed where others had failed primary owing to his ability to listen and empathize with local East Tennesseans.[10] He allowed people gripped by poverty to speak and to be heard. In keeping with the folk school pattern, Horton encouraged the local people to look within their own experiences to devise solutions to the problems of poverty and unemployment. When he founded the Highlander School, one of the first things he did was to let the local people determine the curriculum for the school.[11] As he had learned during his first days in Appalachia as a young man, Horton started with the assumption that locals would know best what they needed. We will have more to say about the Highlander School and Horton's role in other facets of its activities in later chapters. Horton's advocacy on behalf of the poor of Appalachia and his defense of their dignity are some of the many contributions from him that connect with the Old Testament prophetic tradition.

CÉSAR CHÁVEZ

Much of the work César Chávez did in organizing farmworkers brought him into close contact with the widespread poverty among migrant communities in the western US. We noted earlier that Chávez's family had experienced the obstacles created by poverty when they lost the family farm. Similar stories of loss and entrenched poverty multiplied among migrant Latino communities

10. Glen, *Highlander*, 12.

11. Ibid., 20.

in the early twentieth century.[12] Chávez was able to bring that firsthand understanding to his work among migrant laborers in California. Even after he had gained a measure of acceptance in labor relations circles, Chávez sought to distance himself from the respectable, suit-wearing style of many labor leaders in the AFL-CIO (American Federation of Labor–Congress of Industrial Organizations), which he felt alienated them from the poor laborers they represented.[13]

Like Dorothy Day, Chávez sought the aid of the church in addressing the poverty within these communities. In a speech he gave in 1968 at the Second Annual Mexican Conference in Sacramento, Chávez called for the church to embrace a greater role in helping alleviate the suffering of the poor. He noted that "the Catholic Charities, agencies of the Catholic Church, [have] millions of dollars earmarked for the poor. But often the money is spent for food baskets for the needy instead of effective action to eradicate the causes of poverty." Chávez's analysis could be applied more broadly to many entities that operate under the label "Christian charities." His perspective calls for a more comprehensive analysis that far too few people of faith are willing to engage. Churches would do well to probe the deeper causes of poverty rather than merely addressing the needs of poor people on an ad hoc basis. Doing so would begin to alleviate the social apathy that seems to permeate so many communities, even communities of faith in the US.

CONCLUSION

Concern for the poor is a common refrain in the Old Testament legal and prophetic texts. Prophets called for advocacy and protection for poor people who lacked social standing and support over against those who took advantage of them or simply ignored their plight. Dorothy Day, Myles Horton, and César Chávez epitomize

---

12. Bender, *Tierra y Libertad*, 13.

13. Prouty, *César Chávez*, 132.

that perspective in the twentieth century. They constitute a strong voice among modern Christians that parallels this prophetic tradition. As such they provide interesting models for people today who wish to walk in the same path. The determination shared by all three of these figures to address the deeper causes of poverty rather than simply dealing with it on the individual level is an important lesson for everyone today. One of the ways Christian communities can begin to adopt this kind of perspective is to be aware of the needs of working people, a subject we turn to in the next chapter.

6

Concern for Working People

AT THE BEGINNING OF the twentieth century the Triangle Shirtwaist Company was one of five hundred garment factories in New
York. The working conditions there were abysmal and some of the
workers, mostly women, were as young as fourteen. Work weeks
of seventy to eighty hours were common and the owners pressured
everyone to work on Sunday with threats of termination. In the
winter of 1909 some women organized and led a strike to protest
their work environment and the hours. Other garment factory
workers joined them and soon the International Ladies' Garment
Workers' Union had thousands of members. Yet despite their best
efforts to shed light on their predicament, the conditions for the
women in the factories did not change. On March 25, 1911, a fire
broke out on the eighth, ninth, and tenth floors, and since the
doors both opened inward and they had been locked—against the
city codes—the workers were trapped inside. Some were crushed
against the locked doors, some leaped to their death from above
the seventh floor. 146 people died in the fire, and the vast majority
of the victims were the women who were working there. Among
the dead, two were only fourteen years old.

The Triangle Shirtwaist fire was a terrible industrial accident
that could have been avoided. Yet there were many more accidents

like it in the opening decades of the twentieth century in the US. In 1904, 27,000 workers were killed on the job in manufacturing, transport, and agriculture, and by 1914 that number had risen to 35,000.[1] Later in this chapter we will have occasion to examine more examples of worker abuses in US history as we look at those who dedicated their lives to shed light on the problems and worked tirelessly to alleviate them.

Thankfully, labor laws that came about as a result of all these tragedies regulate working conditions with greater effect than a century ago, and child labor laws have protected children from the exploitation that was common at that time. Even so, organizations that keep workers' concerns in front of the public have eroded over the past decades, and many jobs have been outsourced to places that lack the kinds of protections enacted in the US following the abuses of the early twentieth century. Consequently, employees in the US are often afraid to stand up for workers' concerns because of fear of losing their jobs to outsourcing. This situation gives management the upper hand because it guarantees that fewer abuses will be reported. Since outsourced jobs often are not protected by US labor laws, two unfortunate realities obtain: job loss in the US, and job creation abroad in locations where perilous working conditions are legal or simply ignored. The gains in labor relations during the twentieth century in the US remain under threat, and workers in the US and all over the world continue to struggle with these problems. In this chapter we will look at the biblical safeguards for working people promoted in the prophetic tradition, and we will connect this theme to the work of Dorothy Day, Myles Horton, César Chávez, and Martin L. King Jr.

The Old Testament prophetic tradition addresses concerns for working people in a number of ways. To obtain a clearer picture of the biblical perspective on this issue, the prophetic texts must be read within the broader context of legal protection for employees in the rest of the Hebrew Bible. One important example of the biblical advocacy for workers concerns the protection of outsiders. The Hebrew word *ger*, often translated as "sojourner," refers

1. Zinn, *People's History*, 327.

to someone who is not affiliated with one of the tribes of Israel. A sojourner could be a foreigner, or an Israelite living within a tribe to which he or she has no direct familial ties. These sojourners were likely people who were somewhat desperate for employment of some kind. Laws that protect the sojourner are designed to keep outsiders from being exploited as laborers while separated from their kinfolk. Biblical narratives depict sojourners who are forced to abandon their ancestral lands because of drought and famine. The story of Ruth and her mother-in-law Naomi provides a dramatic account of the plight of sojourners. Initially it is Naomi's family that sojourns in Moab during a period of famine in Israel. When the crisis passes, Ruth becomes a sojourner in order to accompany her widowed mother-in-law back to Israel. Abraham's descendants are described this way by God (Gen 15:13), and Moses refers to himself as a sojourner (Exod 2:22; 18:3). Levites are also depicted as sojourners in contexts where they need employment. The biblical traditions depict Levites living among other tribes who support them as they carry out their priestly duties (Judg 17–18). These stories suggest a level of communal concern in Israel's traditions for those who find themselves employed by persons outside their tribe.

Sojourners are also protected in biblical laws, where they are often grouped with others who are at risk of maltreatment. For example, sojourners appear alongside male and female servants in Pentateuchal laws designed to protect workers from harm. Deuteronomy groups the poor person with the sojourner as figures vulnerable to exploitation:

> You shall not oppress a hired servant who is needy and poor ['ani and 'ebyon—the word pair we encountered in the previous chapter] among your brothers or from among the sojourners who are in your land, within your gates. You shall pay his wages on the same day (he works). Do not let the sun set without paying him, because he is poor. (Deut 24:14–15a)

The Ten Commandments include a clause that protects the sojourning outsider from mistreatment. In the Decalogue as it is recorded in the book of Exodus, the commandment regarding the Sabbath stipulates that work cannot be done by any male or female servant—not even the sojourner (Exod 20:10). The parallel version of the Decalogue in Deuteronomy repeats the stipulation from Exodus but adds the line "so that your male servant and your female servant may rest like you" (Deut 20:10). This distinction demonstrates the pronounced humanitarian concern that runs through the Deuteronomic code.[2] Other laws issue a more general warning to employers to be sensitive to the needs of working people. For example, Leviticus specifies that "the wages of a hired servant shall not remain with you all night until the morning" (Lev 19:13). The point here seems to be that hired workers need to be paid in a timely manner—according to this text, on a daily basis. So it is clear that the law seeks to protect wage earners as well as outsiders who are working in Israel in addition to male and female servants.

This legal perspective on the protection of working people is shared by the prophets as well. The prophet Malachi provides this warning from God:

> Then I (God) will draw near to you for judgment. I will be a swift witness against the sorcerers, against the adulterers, against those who swear falsely, against those who oppress the hired person regarding wages, the widow and the orphan, against those who thrust aside the sojourner, and do not fear me, says Yahweh of Hosts. (Mal 3:5)

The same groups who receive protection in the legal texts appear here. The wage earner is placed side by side with widows, orphans, and sojourners. The oppression directed against working people appears to take the form of withholding wages. Additionally, Yahweh is depicted here as a champion of those people. The description of Yahweh as a swift witness paints God as a strong advocate for these people at risk. So the prophetic tradition here speaks out against employers who are not paying their workers what they are due.

2. Nelson, *Deuteronomy*, 10.

A similar concept is expressed by Jeremiah, who warns: "Woe to the one who builds his house without righteousness, and upper rooms without justice, he who makes his neighbor serve for free, and does not give him his wages" (Jer 22:13). Manipulating people to work without pay is clearly condemned.

Ezekiel also has harsh words for those who take advantage of sojourners. After indicting other prophets for whitewashing the people's sinful behavior, Ezekiel says, "The people of the land have practiced extortion and committed robbery. They have oppressed the poor and needy, and have oppressed the sojourner without justice" (Ezek 22:29). The indictment here is more generic regarding the mechanisms of oppression. Although it may simply refer to a general mistreatment of these groups of people, the reference to extortion and robbery in the first line could also indicate a refusal to pay them what they are owed.

A text we examined in the previous chapter is also relevant to our current discussion of the prophetic attitude toward the rights of workers:

> Hear this, you who trample the needy and bring the oppressed of the land to an end, saying, "When will the New Moon be over that we may sell grain, and the Sabbath that we may offer wheat for sale, that we may make the ephah small and the shekel great and deal deceitfully with false balances, that we may buy the poor for silver and the needy for a pair of sandals?" (Amos 8:4–6)

These words from Amos provide an important window into the Israelite practice of limiting the workweek, which is already attested in the eighth century. The prophet's rhetoric indicates that the custom of resting during the Sabbath was also observed during certain celebrations throughout the year. Temporal boundaries protected the worker from employers who demanded longer hours of service. At first glance we might be tempted to focus on these lines as an indictment of the people who are selling the grain or wheat, using faulty measures and unethical business practices. That is surely part of the point Amos is raising. Yet the prophet's interest in the practice of ceasing from labor, seen in the reference to the Sabbath and to New Moon celebrations, suggests that this passage has implications for the employer-employee relationship as well. The voice of complaint in these lines from Amos is that of someone who opposes the shortening of the workweek. The employer sees the religious observance of Sabbaths and New Moons as lost revenue. He is an ancient precursor of Charles Dickens's unrepentant Ebenezer Scrooge, who decried the opportunity costs of holiday leave. The complainant whom Amos criticizes represents someone who not only cheats at business transactions, but also has little regard for the traditional practice of resting from labor on special days during the year.

The Old Testament's stance on the proper treatment of working people is clear. Whether they are sojourners or wage earners or people like the Levites, who are all vulnerable to the demands of their employers, these people are to be treated fairly. The words of the prophets parallel the laws that mandate the benevolent treatment of these groups. The prophetic tradition, therefore, encourages care and concern for working people.

DOROTHY DAY

As we noted at the beginning of this chapter, many working people in America endured abysmal conditions during the early twentieth century. In the absence of workplace oversight and legislation to protect workers, industries and businesses in virtually every field often overstepped what most would consider the line between fair treatment of employees and exploitation. Impassioned critiques of unsafe workplaces included Upton Sinclair's 1905 novel *The Jungle*, which spurred Dorothy Day to found *The Catholic Worker*, the weekly periodical that shed light on deplorable working conditions.

In the spring of 1949 gravediggers affiliated with the CIO (Congress of Industrial Organizations) in Queens went on strike for better working conditions, addressing their grievances to their employer: the Roman Catholic Church, represented by Cardinal Francis Spellman. Cardinal Spellman was a staunch anti-communist and would later strongly support Senator Joseph McCarthy's efforts to ferret out and blacklist all suspected communists in the US. Anyone who called for workers' rights was suspect in Spellman's eyes. Instead of addressing the men with understanding, Spellman refused their requests and recruited students from St. Joseph's Seminary to serve as strikebreakers. Eventually the cardinal wore down the workers and broke their strike. Yet Cardinal Spellman's victory was not complete. Day advocated for the gravediggers by exposing their struggle and the church's role in the conflict in the *Catholic Worker*, much to the dismay of the cardinal.

During the Great Depression, Dorothy Day and Peter Maurin sought to build a network of farms on Staten Island, in upstate New York, and in eastern Pennsylvania in order to provide paying jobs for people out of work because of the economy. Maurin convinced Day of the importance of these farms, which reflected a tradition of subsistence farming he had learned in Canada under Pyotr Kropotkin. Day did not view these farms as a venture separate from her work. Instead, she saw them as rural versions of the houses of hospitality she had established. The farms were another way to help people without robbing them of their dignity, and they also helped sustain the kitchens in the urban houses of hospitality. During World War II these farms also provided employment opportunities for people who, acting on their conscience, did not want to work in any industry that directly assisted the war effort. Day and Maurin thus cultivated a pacifist community at a time when public support for the war was at its zenith.

MYLES HORTON

Like Dorothy Day and Peter Maurin, Myles Horton was concerned about poor people in general and the working poor in particular. His Highlander School addressed a deep need in the South from its very first days. In previous decades, numerous attempts to improve working conditions in the region had been made. Yet the coal magnates relied on the support of the state government to break strikes by using inmates from state penitentiaries. In the 1890s corporations like Tennessee Coal and Iron would lease inmates from the state prisons for a pittance to replace striking workers, eroding the collective strength of the strike and silencing the voice of the miners. This practice resulted in a series of clashes in August 1892 in Grundy County. Miners had grown tired of the strategy of using inmates to replace them when they complained about working conditions. These miners organized and marched on the prison in nearby Tracy City. The men took control of the prison, marched the prisoners out, loaded them onto a freight train, and ordered the conductor to take them to Nashville. The miners then set fire to the stockade, burning it to the ground. Word of the incident spread throughout the region and other miners were emboldened to confront similar situations in their own mines. Eventually the state militia was brought in to quell the uprisings but the miners' actions had set in motion the wheels of change. In 1899 the Tennessee state legislature outlawed the practice of leasing out prisoners to the mining corporations. Even so, the concerns of working people were still a low priority within industry and in the mind of the population at large. Miners continued to work in dangerously deplorable conditions. This is the historical backdrop of Myles Horton's work in Grundy County and the surrounding areas of East Tennessee.

Soon after opening the Highlander Folk School, Horton went to nearby Wilder in Fentress County, where another group of miners was trying to organize a strike in the summer of 1932. The men were being paid in scrip that was only good at the company store, where prices were higher than local stores. The company also deducted from the miners' wages for company housing and other services that were not actually provided. Many of the miners were in debt to the store and could not leave their jobs. The strike continued into the winter and the company leveraged the cold weather by cutting off the electricity to the company housing and removing the doors of the houses. The governor ordered National Guard troops in after an old trestle was destroyed by an explosion. The Red Cross was called in, but the local Red Cross chairperson was the wife of the mine superintendent. So none of the aid reached the families of the striking workers, who were starving and suffering from the cold.[3]

In response, Horton organized food drives to provide for the families in Wilder and eventually he was arrested by a National Guard officer. When Horton asked what the charges against him were, the officer replied, "For coming here and getting information and going back [to Highlander] and teaching it."[4] This was the first time Horton had been arrested and he noted later that this was the only time the charges against him were correct—gathering and spreading information was exactly what he was doing at Wilder and Highlander.[5] In addition to being arrested, Horton and numerous members of Highlander received death threats throughout the strike. The strike was finally broken when the leader, Barney Graham, was shot and the strikers' families were forcibly removed from company housing. The defeat of the strikers illustrates just how powerful corporate management was in the early days of Highlander. Although his advocacy on behalf of the workers in Wilder ultimately proved unsuccessful, Horton convinced Dr. Arthur Morgan, the head of the newly created Tennessee Valley Authority to hire as many of the ousted strikers as possible to work on local TVA projects.

When Highlander opened its doors in 1932 the region of East Tennessee was in the midst of a lumber boom: corporations were sweeping into the region and clear-cutting all the timber. Yet once the clear-cutting was complete, the corporations moved on and the jobs went with them. As in the 1890s, the concerns of working people were overridden by those of industry. In 1933, a year after the Wilder coal miners' strike, Myles Horton and the staff at Highlander became involved in the Bugwood cutters strike in Grundy County. The striking woodcutters partnered with Highlander and formed the Cumberland Mountain Workers and Unemployed League. Picket lines were set up around the forests where the men

3. Adams, *Unearthing Seeds of Fire*, 31.

4. Ibid., 32.

5. Horton, interview with Bill Moyers.

had worked. The lumber company sent out men to intimidate the strikers, telling them that their strike was illegal. Yet the men had learned from the staff at Highlander that the National Industrial Recovery Act guaranteed workers the right to bargain collectively. While the strike ultimately was unsuccessful, the people of Grundy County began to see that they could organize and speak to problems in their region. They could do so despite anti-union personalities like wool magnate John Edgerton, who fought to deny federal funds to Highlander, and church leaders like Billy Sunday, who preached against Highlander, accusing it of promoting communism.[6] Experiences like this led Horton to see how the power structures of wealth and industry were propped up by churches. Everywhere Horton went he met resistance from churches and community leaders who backed industry and business.

Undaunted by such efforts, Highlander continued its mission and was also instrumental in helping working people during World War II and thereafter. Between 1942 and 1947 the American labor movement was growing steadily. Yet in the South there were obstacles to worker protection, as indicated by the strikes in Wilder and in Grundy County and these obstacles proved effective for opponents of the labor movement. Less than one-fourth of the members of the AFL (American Federation of Labor) and less than one-tenth of the members of the CIO (Congress of Industrial Organizations) were from the South. Southern state legislatures sought to undermine attempts to unionize, and during the war, work stoppages were considered unpatriotic. Thus, labor representation faced a number of hurdles during the 1940s.

In September 1943, Horton went to help ease racial tensions at the Rohm and Haas Plexiglas factory in Knoxville through "personal work" with black and white leaders in the plant. During this time Highlander became a CIO school, and the UAW (Union of Auto Workers) held workshops there in June 1944—the first occasion on which black and white people attended the same classes in a Southern labor school.[7] In the same year representatives from

6. Adams, *Unearthing Seeds of Fire*, 39.

7. Glen, *Highlander*, 106.

other unions came to Highlander—the Mine, Mill, and Smelter Workers, the United Furniture Workers of America, and the Glass, Ceramic, and Silica Sand Workers.

After the war the need for organization increased again in the face of staunch opposition to the labor movement. As the US was moving away from a war economy and soldiers were returning to the labor force, people began to blame inflation and other economic woes on the labor movement. This sentiment, coupled with an increasing fear of any group that appeared sympathetic to communist ideas, led to the Taft-Hartley Act of 1947, which severely restricted the power of organized labor.

As time marched on and Highlander continued to work on labor issues, its focus turned more and more toward race relations. Horton and the other leaders at Highlander came to realize that race and labor were intertwined in many ways; working on one without the other could never be fully effective in achieving goals such as equal pay for equal work irrespective of one's skin color. From the beginning, meetings at Highlander ignored the Jim Crow laws regarding segregation, much to the dismay of some local leaders. All meetings were open to anyone of any race who wanted to learn. Highlander became a place for people to strategize about how to respond to racism and segregation, and during the 1950s people began coming to Highlander to learn the techniques of nonviolent resistance and organized civil disobedience. The list of individuals who came to Highlander for these purposes reads like a veritable "who's who" of the civil rights movement and includes John Lewis, James Bevell, Ralph Abernathy, Martin L. King Jr., and Rosa Parks. In fact, Parks had been at Highlander just a few weeks before she refused to surrender her seat on a Montgomery bus in December 1955.

As the civil rights movement gained momentum in a number of states, Southern political bosses began to seek ways to thwart its advance. As a result, the Highlander Folk School and Myles Horton became targets of McCarthy's "red scare" witch hunt. Southern politicians used the accusation of communism to veil their disdain for Highlander's work on behalf of labor and its participation in the civil rights movement. Horton was subpoenaed to testify before the Eastland Senate Committee (named for Senator James Eastland from Mississippi) and faced potential charges of contempt of Congress for refusing to testify about anyone besides himself. In the late 1950s the ubiquitous concern about pervasive communism led to efforts to revoke the state charter for the Highlander School in Monteagle and to padlock the buildings. As the FBI shuttered the few buildings at the school, Horton stood in the parking lot laughing and said, "You can't padlock an idea."[8] Eventually Horton moved the school closer to Knoxville and reopened it under a new name, the Highlander Research and Education Center. He continued the mission of the school well into his old age, continuing to tackle labor issues and racism worldwide. Horton's commitment to speaking the truth about the plight of working people and their basic civil rights, to putting those words into action, and to courageously facing the consequences makes him an inspiring model for walking in the prophetic tradition.

CÉSAR CHÁVEZ

Like Day and Horton, César Chávez recognized the struggle of US workers in the twentieth century and took action. As the son of migrant workers, Chávez had firsthand experience with the difficulties that impoverished people working on farms faced. In the wake of the National Labor Relations Act in 1935, many workers in the US were allowed to form unions and collectively bargain with their employers. The act did not extend to agricultural workers, however, so the average farm laborer had no way to redress matters of intolerable workplace conditions and insufficient compensation. This particular inequity led Chávez and Delores Huerta to organize the National Farmworkers Association in 1962, which later became the United Farm Workers. At their very first meeting they committed to advocate for a minimum wage for farmworkers.

Within three years Chávez led the UFW in its first strike against grape growers in Delano, California. Chávez garnered such

8. See Schneider, *You Can't Padlock an Idea.*

attention during this strike that New York senator (and former attorney general) Robert F. Kennedy came to lend support. Kennedy held a public hearing in Delano for the Senate Subcommittee on Migratory Labor the day before the scheduled UFW march. A comical exchange ensued between Kennedy and the sheriff of Kern County, Leroy Galyen. The sheriff claimed that if he had reason to believe that a riot was about to start, he would arrest the people who were demonstrating. Kennedy asked him if he would charge them with a crime. "Yes," replied the sheriff, "charge them with unlawful assemblage." Kennedy then asked how he knew that these demonstrators were planning to start a riot. Sheriff Galyen replied that some of the men in the field told the police that if the demonstrators were not removed, they were "going to cut their hearts out." The sheriff claimed that he was protecting the demonstrators by arresting them, claiming that "rather than let them get cut, you should remove the cause [of the riot]." In response the senator asked, "How can you arrest someone when they haven't violated the law?" Sheriff Galyen responded, "They're ready to violate the law." At this point the crowd broke into raucous laughter. Kennedy concluded by saying, "Could I suggest in the interim period of time, in the luncheon period of time, that the sheriff and the attorney general [of Kern County] read the Constitution of the United States?"[9] This moment galvanized the UFW and energized the marchers led by Chávez the next day. In the minds of many of the marchers this support from Senator Kennedy marked the first time an elected official had advocated on their behalf.

The Senate hearings and the march from Delano to Sacramento were the first of several actions that César Chávez and the UFW undertook on behalf of working people. Even at the end of his life Chávez was still organizing laborers. The Wrath of Grapes campaign, a movement to address the use of pesticides that harmed the men and women working in these fields, was in full swing when he died in his sleep in 1993.

9. A full account of the hearings and of the arrests of striking workers in the weeks preceding the hearings can be found in Bender, *One Night in America*, 15–18. Edited video clips of the interchange during the hearing are widely available on YouTube.

MARTIN L. KING JR.

In addition to civil rights, Martin L. King Jr. was committed to shedding light on the plight of working people. In the very last speech he gave before he was assassinated on April 4, 1968, King addressed a Memphis crowd on behalf of the city's sanitation workers. The workers had gone on strike on February 12, 1968, walking off the job to protest widespread discrimination in the sanitation department and dangerous working conditions. The walkout was triggered by the deaths of two sanitation workers, Echol Cole and Robert Walker, who were crushed to death in a garbage truck when they sought refuge during a rainstorm. The department had forbidden workers from seeking shelter in any other place besides the truck during periods of rain. Cole and Walker climbed into the back part of the garbage truck to escape the rain and were crushed by the compacting mechanism.

King decided to go to Memphis to shed light on the sanitation workers' grievances. At a demonstration on March 28, protesters began breaking windows and the police responded with force, killing one demonstrator. On April 3, in a speech at the Mason Temple, the headquarters of the Church of God in Christ, King said:

> The issue is injustice. The issue is the refusal of Memphis to be fair and honest in its dealings with its public servants, who happen to be sanitation workers. Now we've got to keep attention on that. That's always the problem with a little violence. You know what happened the other day, and the press dealt only with the window-breaking. I read the articles. They very seldom got around to mentioning the fact that one thousand, three hundred sanitation workers were on strike, and that Memphis is not being fair to them. . . . They didn't get around to that. Now we're going to march again, and we've got to march again, in order to put the issue where it is supposed to be. And force everybody to see that there are thirteen hundred of God's children here suffering, sometimes going hungry, going through dark and dreary nights wondering how this thing is going to come out. That's the issue.

And we've got to say to the nation: we know it's coming out. For when people get caught up with that which is right and they are willing to sacrifice for it, there is no stopping point short of victory.[10]

We can only wonder how King would have expanded his efforts to support working people had he lived. His words and presence in Memphis in April 1968 demonstrated his commitment to working people under the banner of civil rights and shed light on how the vile practice of racism was manifested in the thoughtless exploitation of workers.

CONCLUSION

The prophetic tradition stresses fair treatment of working people, a theme found in Old Testament narratives, legal texts, and the prophetic books. Not surprisingly, the theme extends to the New Testament as well. In the Epistle of James we read:

> Come now, you rich people, weep and wail for the miseries that are coming to you. Your riches have rotted, and your clothes are moth-eaten. Your gold and silver have rusted, and their rust will be evidence against you and it will eat your flesh like fire. You have laid up treasure for the last days. Listen, the wages of the workers who mowed your fields, which you kept back by dishonesty, cry out, and the cries of the harvesters have reached the ears of the Lord of Hosts. (Jas 5:1–4)

Day, Horton, Chávez, and King spoke with a unified voice in their support of workers, echoing in the twentieth century the message expressed by the biblical prophets. The way we treat working people matters, and advocacy on their behalf is another way to live out the Old Testament prophetic tradition.

---

10. King, "I See the Promised Land," 281.

7

Concern for Justice

"WE WANT JUSTICE." IN countless contexts people who feel as though they have been wronged express this demand. While the quest for justice is surely a widespread cultural value throughout the world, we in the US pride ourselves on the notion that justice will prevail. Such claims can be detected in a number of our national slogans. In the preamble to the US Constitution, the founding fathers aspire to "establish justice and insure domestic tranquility." The Pledge of Allegiance ends with the phrase "liberty and justice for all." Although there might be debate about the precise ways in which justice should be carried out, it is clear that the vast majority of people in the US want justice to prevail. But imagine an Ivy League professor walking into a college classroom and posing the following scenario:

> You are a driver of a streetcar that has begun to roll down a hill and the brakes have failed. Ahead the tracks divide so that you are faced with two—and only two—options. You can keep the car on the current track and crash into a group of five people who are working on the track or you can turn the car and crash into one person. What is the right thing to do? What is the *just* course of action?[1]

---

1. Michael Sandel, professor of political philosophy at Harvard, has made his undergraduate course on justice widely available online. A number of the

Many of the students respond that crashing into one person is better than crashing into a group, suggesting that it is better that one die rather than five. The professor then poses another scenario:

> A physician has a group of patients who desperately need various organ transplants in order to survive. Each needs a separate organ—one a heart, one a kidney, etc. She also has a relatively healthy patient who needs a simple procedure that will involve full sedation. This healthy patient just happens to be a perfect match for a transplant procedure for each of the group who face imminent death without a transplant. Could the doctor simply take the organs from the relatively healthy patient while the patient was under anesthesia and give them to each member of the group who will die if they do not receive a transplant?

Many students who supported the action of steering the streetcar into the individual in order to save the group of workers are not as enthusiastic about the doctor's plan to harvest organs from relatively healthy patients. Both scenarios provide a way to question the notion of utility. When is it "just" to save a group at the expense of an individual?

These are just some of the many ways in which the discussion of "justice" in our world can be challenging. In a college classroom there may be deep disagreement over constructing a just approach to the hypothetical scenarios. Students might come from various faith traditions or no faith tradition at all. Among such varied points of view, how can people claim to know what is just and act accordingly, and call others to act accordingly?

Increasingly in the last few decades the conversation about ethics and justice has centered around communities. These "communitarian-based ethics" constitute a reaction to the classical liberal position that assumes that the rights of an individual overrule community opinion. The right thing to do in a given situation is assumed to be communally determined rather than derived from

---

lectures begin with scenarios like this one designed to help students think about notions of correct behavior.

abstract principles that transcend cultures. Ethical approaches and strategies for establishing justice can be shaped by a people's identity, traditions, and views of ultimate reality, such as its concept of God. In this recent conversation, the individual, rational subject who was the traditional protagonist in Western Enlightenment thought is no longer viewed as an independent agent who determines how to answer questions of justice. Justice is conceived as communally derived, conditioned by what a given community assumes to be rational.

Michael Sandel establishes a middle ground between these two opposing viewpoints, one that avoids the problems of each. Consider Sandel's helpful illustration from his book *Liberalism and the Limits of Justice*:[2] he juxtaposes the rights of two groups who sought to hold a demonstration in a US city. On the one side are the Neo-Nazis who claimed the right to march in Skokie, Illinois, where a number of Holocaust survivors lived. On the other side Sandel places the marches associated with Martin Luther King Jr. that were staged in a number of cities in the American South. The classic liberal position would elevate the right to march above all community concerns. Therefore, according to this point of view, each group should be given the right to march irrespective of the way the community's citizens feel about the ideology of the group. The communitarian position, on the other hand, would suggest that neither group should be able to march because in each case, the community in which the marchers are embedded has a prior claim, rooted in history and cultural viewpoint, that finds their ideology offensive. I suspect that neither of these positions would be favored by most readers of this book—people who, in the main, would grant King's group the freedom to march while denying such a right to the Neo-Nazis. Sandel's middle-ground approach suggests that one could argue in defense of King's group. He notes that the obvious ground for distinguishing the cases is that neo-Nazis promote genocide and hate, whereas King sought civil rights for black people. Sandel further argues that there is also a difference in the moral worth of the communities whose integrity is at

2. Sandel, *Liberalism*, ix --- xvi.

stake—the shared memories of the Holocaust survivor deserve a moral deference that the solidarity of the segregationists does not.

The solution that Sandel outlines is akin to the approach I would take to the notion of justice that the biblical prophets invoke. Justice is not an abstract individual right that automatically trumps community concerns. Neither is justice a mere cultural construct. Justice is derived partly from each but it also arises within the human understanding of moral discourse. Justice partakes of abstract notions as well as community mores, but there is also an inner conviction about what is right that is relevant too. When confronted with Neo-Nazis and Freedom Riders, most humans have a similar feeling about who is in the right. In this chapter I argue that the biblical notion of justice is treated by the prophets as a similar kind of moral discernment. The prophets do not provide a manual of behavior in which abstract ethical principles are categorized and labeled in encyclopedic fashion. The prophets were communally based and they approached questions of "doing the right thing" within the matrix of being the people of Yahweh.

Yet the prophets also knew the people whom they addressed, and we will see that their call for justice is rooted in the assumption that the right thing to do is something that most discerning communities instinctively know and feel or can be led to understand and embrace.

OLD TESTAMENT DISCOURSE

The call for justice has deep biblical roots and constitutes another prominent theme in the words of the Old Testament prophets, a point long recognized by many biblical scholars. In what follows I want to take a moment to examine the Hebrew words used by the prophets to denote the concept of justice.

There are several words in Biblical Hebrew that can be translated with the English word "justice." The most frequent of these terms is *mishpaṭ*, which can signify "a judgment," or a decision in a particular case; "a matter under judgment"; or, more abstractly, "what is determined by judges and lawgivers, what is right, justice."

It is the third definition, with an emphasis on the phrase "what is right," that is most appropriate for contexts in which the prophets call for justice. A thorough word study of a number of prophetic texts that employ the word *mishpaṭ* in this sense will prove helpful to the way one thinks about responding to the biblical call for justice. The following paragraphs will consider how justice is depicted in the books of Isaiah, Jeremiah, Ezekiel, Hosea, Amos, and Micah to arrive at an adequate sampling of the biblical picture.

In Isaiah the word *mishpaṭ* appears forty-three times. In the early chapters of Isaiah the people are called to "seek *mishpaṭ*" (1:17; 16:5), while in later chapters God speaks of his servant "bringing *mishpaṭ*" (42:1, 3) or "keeping *mishpaṭ*" (56:1). Most importantly, *mishpaṭ* often appears in poetic parallel with *tsedaqah* or *tsedeq*, which both mean "righteousness" (1:21, 27; 5:7; 9:6 [Eng v. 7], 16; 16:5; 26:9; 28:17; 32:1,16; 33:5; 59:14). We noted in an earlier chapter that poetic parallelism is important to consider when determining the precise meaning of a given word in the Old Testament. Poetic parallelism often indicates a synonymous relationship between two terms. Thus, when *mishpaṭ* appears in parallel with "righteousness" (*tsedaqah*), this is a strong indication that *mishpaṭ* is closely related to the concept of righteousness. When all the occurrences of *mishpaṭ* in Isaiah are considered, the word can clearly refer in some contexts to a legal sense of justice (10:2) or to judgments (34:5; 53:8; 54:17). The majority of the occurrences of *mishpaṭ*, however, could be easily understood as signifying "what is right," and the commands to enact *mishpaṭ* certainly denote this latter meaning. The prophetic command in Isaiah is best summarized in the following command: "Learn to do good, seek justice, correct oppression, defend the fatherless, plead for the orphan" (Isa 1:17).

In Jeremiah the word *mishpaṭ* occurs thirty-one times, and in fifteen cases it clearly refers to punishment, legal or divine (Jer 1:16; 4:12; 5:28; 12:1; 26:11, 16; 30:18; 32:7, 8; 39:5; 48:21, 47; 49:12; 51:9; 52:9). Of the remaining sixteen occurrences of the word in Jeremiah, most are found in contexts where the people are called to "do *mishpaṭ*" with their fellow Israelites (7:5; 9:23; 22:3,

15; 23:5, 33:15), and *mishpaṭ* is often coupled with "righteousness" (*tsedaqah*) in poetic parallel (4:2; 9:23; 22:3, 15; 23:5, 33:15), as we saw in Isaiah. Warnings against not acting "with/in keeping with *mishpaṭ*" appear in Jeremiah as well, for example: "Woe to him who builds his house without righteousness and an upper room without *mishpaṭ*" (Jer 22:13). Further, "Like a partridge that gathers a brood which she did not hatch is one who gets rich not by *mishpaṭ*" (Jer 17:11). Clearly Jeremiah can use the term *mishpaṭ* to speak of right and proper living too.

The word appears forty-three times in Ezekiel and on twenty-six occasions refers to a type of law or statute, usually rendered "ordinance" in English Bibles. Most of the remaining uses of *mishpaṭ* in Ezekiel refer to proper action. The word is in poetic parallel with "righteousness" (*tsedaqah*) eight times (18:5, 19, 21, 27; 33:14, 16, 19; 45:9) and spoken of as something that is "done," a locution often seen in Isaiah and Jeremiah as well. This meaning is illustrated nicely in the phrase, "a righteous man will do true justice person to person" (Ezek 18:8).

Hosea employs the word *mishpaṭ* six times, mostly with the meaning of judgment or punishment (Hos 5:1, 11; 6:5; 10:4). Twice the word indicates proper conduct—just living. Yahweh says, "I will betroth you to me in righteousness (*tsedeq*) and *mishpaṭ*" (Hos 2:19 [v. 21 in Hebrew]), and he commands the people to "hold fast to love and *mishpaṭ*" (12:6 [v. 7 in Hebrew]).

The prophet Amos uses the word *mishpaṭ* four times. Twice Amos warns against turning *mishpaṭ* into poison (6:12) or bitterness (5:7), and in each case *mishpaṭ* is paired with "righteousness" (*tsedaqah*). On another occasion Amos calls the people to "hate evil, love good, [and] establish *mishpaṭ* at the gate" (Amos 5:15). As we have noted in earlier chapters, the reference to the gate here likely refers to judicial decisions that were handed down at the entrance to cities and towns in ancient Israel. Amos's support of the poor elsewhere indicates that this call for justice refers to right judgement for those who lack economic or social support. In perhaps the most famous reference to justice in Amos, the prophet says, "Let *mishpaṭ* roll down like waters and righteousness (*tsedaqah*) like an ever-flowing stream" (Amos 5:24). Amos's use of *mishpaṭ* mirrors what we have seen in Isaiah, Jeremiah, and Ezekiel: right and proper conduct in general and in legal matters in particular.

Among the words of the prophet Micah, the word *mishpaṭ* appears five times. Micah's use of the word is similar to the other prophets surveyed thus far. Yet Micah pairs the term with "upright conduct" (Hebrew *yesharah*) when he chides the rulers of Israel as ones who "abhor *mishpaṭ* and pervert upright conduct" (Mic 3:9). In 3:1 Micah accuses these same leaders, saying, "Are you not supposed to know *mishpaṭ*?" Micah also speaks of "doing *mishpaṭ*" (6:8) in conjunction with loving kindness and walking humbly with God. Elsewhere a repentant Israel cries out to God to "do justice for me" (Mic 7:9). Yet again, the notion of *mishpaṭ* as "doing what is right" is fully in line with the prophetic idiom outlined in the examples above.

The preceding survey demonstrates the pervasive use of the word *mishpaṭ* by many of the prophets to indicate justice in the sense of proper conduct or right behavior. So when one thinks about how to apply the calls for justice seen among these prophets, one must think beyond a legal sense and understand the concept as doing the right thing. Seeking justice in Hebrew is closer to our notion of discernment followed by enaction —the act of determining what the proper action would be and then implementing it. In the biblical context, as noted above, seeking justice requires engaging in fair dealings with the poor and with people without familial advocacy, such as widows and orphans. Making sure that the right things are done for those people at risk is of fundamental concern for the spokesmen of the God of Israel.

MARTIN L. KING JR.

The concept of justice cannot be discussed in the contemporary context without mentioning Dr. Martin Luther King Jr., whose name is intricately linked with the civil rights movement and nonviolent resistance to racism in America. Martin King is rightly recognized for his deep commitment to justice and the heroic way he dedicated his life to calling people to do the right thing, to act properly in the biblical sense. Although it has taken some time for a consensus on this assessment to emerge in America,[3] King's role in calling the US to live up to its ideals is unmatched in the twentieth century.

As a child growing up in Atlanta, Martin King knew the intricate workings of the segregated South and how it divided people by skin color into various levels of citizenship in a de facto sense. Racism, W. E. B. Du Bois's notion of "the problem of the color line," permeated everything throughout the US but particularly so in the Old South, the states that comprised the Confederacy in the nineteenth century. To illustrate King's commitment to justice in step with the Old Testament prophetic tradition, we will focus upon major statements he made on four occasions: during the Montgomery Bus Boycott, during his incarceration in the Birmingham city jail, at the Southern Christian Leadership Conference in 1967, and at the University of California at Berkeley in 1957.

King's public role in confronting the Jim Crow system of segregation had its genesis in the Montgomery Bus Boycott, which began in December 1955 and extended to the fall of 1956. The Montgomery Improvement Association, comprised of local African American citizens, was organized to address racial injustice in that city. The group's slogan was "Justice without Violence." King's insistence on nonviolence was deeply rooted in his assumptions about justice and transcendent faith. "The method of nonviolence," he said, "is based on the conviction that the universe is on the side of justice. It is this deep faith in the future that causes the nonviolent resister to accept suffering without retaliation. He knows that in his struggle for justice he has cosmic companionship."[4]

The catalyst against the injustice in Montgomery was the courageous action of Mrs. Rosa Parks, who had been selected by

3. The federal holiday named for Martin Luther King Jr., signed into law in November 1983 and celebrated for the first time in 1986, was not recognized in Arizona until 1992 and in South Carolina not until 2000.

4. King, "Nonviolence and Racial Justice," 9.

Montgomery organizers to provoke a challenge to the legality of the segregation of city buses. (Months earlier, Parks had traveled to the Highlander Folk School led by Myles Horton to learn the ways of civil disobedience.) She refused to yield her seat to a white bus rider and was arrested. King was selected to be the spokesperson for the boycott and so began his career of persuading America to live up to its ideals concerning the fair treatment of its citizens. In his 1956 reflections on the boycott, King noted that this direct action was an early attempt to move African American people away from a stoic approach that quietly "accepted injustice, insult, injury and exploitation." He characterized the challenges in Montgomery as more than mere racial tension. For King,

> the tension in this city is not between white people and Negro people. The tension is at bottom between justice and injustice, between the forces of light and the forces of darkness. And if there is a victory it will be a victory not merely for fifty thousand Negroes, but a victory for justice and the forces of light. We are out to defeat injustice and not white persons who may happen to be unjust.[5]

When twenty-four Christian ministers were arrested on February 22, 1956, for participating in the nonviolent protest in support of the bus boycott, their slogan became "It is an honor to face jail for a just cause." In a sermon that he preached on November 6, 1956, one week before the U.S. Supreme Court ruled against Alabama's bus segregation laws, King connected his vision of justice with love for the ones committing injustice. On that day he enjoined his audience, "As you press on for justice, be sure to move with dignity and discipline, using only the weapon of love. Let no man pull you so low as to hate him. Always avoid violence."[6] King concluded in his reflections on that pivotal year by saying, "We believe that if the method we use in dealing with equality in the buses can eliminate injustice in ourselves, we shall at the same time be attacking the basis of injustice—man's hostility to man."[7] The boycott under

5. Ibid., 8.
6. King, "Most Durable Power," 10.
7. King, "Our Struggle," 81.

King's leadership came to a successful conclusion on December 20, 1956, when the city passed an ordinance overturning the Jim Crow seating arrangements. King's "Letter from Birmingham Jail" should be required reading for every person of faith. This letter, written by King on April 16, 1963, after he had been arrested during a march and imprisoned, was originally addressed to seven Christian clergy and one rabbi. This text serves as a cautionary tale, illustrating how one's religious sensibilities can cloud proper thinking. The ministers to whom this letter was addressed were not vicious racists. They were actually more liberal-minded than most people in the city where they worked. Yet they, too, were not speaking and acting properly and they deserved the censure they received in this letter.

In the letter King made a number of references to justice and injustice. Early in his missive King penned the famous line, "Injustice anywhere is a threat to justice everywhere."[8] This statement was King's response to the accusation that he had been an outsider who had come to Alabama to stir up trouble. Yet he explained that he had been invited by the churches to help them deal with the injustice of their plight. King's letter also referred to unjust laws that must be disobeyed by just people. His accusers had accused him of hypocrisy, since he and other civil rights leaders had gone to jail for violating laws while also calling for the enforcement of legal pronouncements such as *Brown v. Board of Education*, the Supreme Court case that struck down the notion of "separate but equal" and paved the way for the integration of public schools. King addressed the accusation of hypocrisy by defining some laws as just and others as unjust. As a biblical precedent, King cited from the book of Daniel (3:16–17) the example of Shadrach, Meshach, and Abednego, who refused to obey the law of Nebuchadnezzar, king of Babylon, when it violated their consciences. In a similar vein King noted that everything Hitler did in Nazi Germany was "legal." So what is just and what is legal are by no means one and the same.

8. King, "Letter from Birmingham City Jail," 290.

Another memorable line from this letter concerns the power of justice and what is right: "Right defeated is stronger than evil triumphant." It is a line that King used again later in his Nobel Prize acceptance speech. This declaration illustrates the deep level of hope King exhibited in his commitment to justice. Even in defeat, those who are in the right triumph. It is truly a remarkable line, one that clearly resonated with those who had worked for years, sometimes a lifetime, for civil rights. In his Nobel speech, King added the word "temporarily" just before "defeated" to indicate his confidence that right would not ultimately be defeated.

In keeping with this sentiment is an expression from a speech entitled "Where Do We Go from Here?" that King delivered before the Southern Christian Leadership Conference in 1967. Near the end of the speech he said, "Let us realize that the arc of the moral universe is long but it bends toward justice." King borrowed this line from the nineteenth-century abolitionist minister Theodore Parker. Again, King's citation of Parker depicts the hopeful outlook that King carried with him, a hope that what is right would eventually be embraced by all in the arc of human existence.

Despite his generally hopeful outlook, King was all too aware of the challenges to justice that persisted. In a speech at the University of California at Berkeley on June 4, 1957, he noted the importance of a willingness to fall out of step with modern culture in order to stand against injustice as the prophets of old did.

> Modern psychology has a word that is probably used more than any other word. It is the word "maladjusted." Now we all should seek to live a well-adjusted life in order to avoid neurotic and schizophrenic personalities. But there are some things within our social order to which I am proud to be maladjusted and to which I call upon you to be maladjusted. I never intend to adjust myself to segregation and discrimination. I never intend to adjust myself to mob rule. I never intend to adjust myself to the tragic effects of the methods of physical violence and to tragic militarism. I call upon you to be maladjusted to such things. I call upon you to be as maladjusted as Amos who in the midst of the injustices of his day cried

out in words that echo across the generation, "Let judgment run down like waters, and righteousness like a
mighty stream."[9]

King shows that it is a perennial challenge to stand against the
cultural tides, and to turn a critical eye upon one's own thinking in
order to ferret out how cultural baggage can produce blind spots
that lead to injustice and subtle complicity with injustice.

CONCLUSION

The biblical prophets were clearly concerned about justice. Their
call for right behavior does not allude to an abstract principle nor
to a communally derived cultural outlook. The prophets assume
that the people of God have a sense of what is right. The commitment to justice seen in Isaiah, Jeremiah, Ezekiel, Hosea, Amos, and
Micah was fully embraced and perhaps best illustrated by Martin
Luther King Jr. The speeches King gave all over the US continue
to inspire people today. He is rightly recognized as one of the pre-
miere orators of the twentieth century. Yet King's speeches were
more than oratorical art. They exemplified a commitment to what
is right and the courage to tell the truth to the powers that be,
whether cultural or political. King denounced the injustice of the
Jim Crow tradition, a stance that cut against the grain in much of
the US in the 1960s. King denounced the injustice of the Vietnam
War long before it was acceptable to do so. He saw in the Vietnamese people the plight of African Americans in the US. On the
day he was assassinated, April 4, 1968, King was about to give a
speech in support of the sanitation workers in Memphis, who were
organizing a strike to bring about more just working conditions.
Addressing these themes so openly was dangerous, and ultimately
proved deadly for King. Yet such an approach is in step with the
biblical prophetic tradition, as we will see in the next chapter.

9. King, "Power of Nonviolence," 14. King repeated these lines in a com-
mencement speech he gave at Lincoln University in Pennsylvania on June 6,
1961. See King, "American Dream," 216.

8

Courageous Risk

In 1402 a Catholic priest named Jan Hus (1370–1415) began preaching in Prague, condemning the moral failings of priests, bishops, and the pope. Hus had studied the works of John Wycliff (1330–1384), who decades earlier had questioned these issues of the church as well. During Hus's lifetime the leadership of the church was bitterly contested and a number of men vied for the title of pope. One group of cardinals had elected Urban VI while others chose Clement VII, and in the wake of these conflicts armed forces were raised by opposing sides, often financed with church taxes and monies gained from selling absolutions and other ecclesial favors.[1] The schism continued among the successors of the rival popes until 1409, when the warring factions were brought together under a new pope, Alexander V. Yet the arrangement was short-lived. One of the cardinals, Baldassare Cossa, who served the new pope as his principal councillor, was rumored to have poisoned his master; Cossa succeeded Alexander V under the papal name John XXIII.[2] In order to raise money to supply his army so as to defend his control over church holdings, John XXIII

1. Lützow, *Life and Times of John Hus*, 94.

2. Ibid., 95; he is not to be confused with the twentieth-century Pope John XXIII.

issued papal bulls that granted remission of sins to those who were contrite and who were willing to equip and support a soldier for a month.[3] This act had the appearance of simony—the practice of selling spiritual favors—and it established a foundation for the tradition of selling indulgences, an abuse that Martin Luther would address about a century later.

The papal rivalries and self-serving abuses, coupled with the teachings of Wycliff regarding the use of vernacular languages (rather than Latin) at Mass and the necessity of making the Bible available in translation to all, spawned a reform movement that gained momentum in some areas of Europe. This was the backdrop for the work of Jan Hus. By 1415 Hus had stirred up quite a controversy in the Czech lands with his pro-Wycliff sympathies. That same year the young priest was invited to the city of Constance, on the border between modern Germany and Switzerland, to appear at a church council, and his safety was guaranteed by Sigismund of Hungary, the Holy Roman Emperor at the time. But the invitation was a trap and Hus was arrested and thrown into a dungeon and nearly starved, against the protestations of Sigismund.[4] At his trial Hus stood by his reformist positions, promising to recant anything if it did not conform to the teachings of the Bible. On July 6, 1415, Jan Hus was condemned for heresy when he refused to recant his teachings, and he was burned at the stake. Upon hearing his sentence, Hus prayed before the council that God would forgive his enemies. Hus is rightly recognized as one of the first Reformers, providing a bridge between Wycliff and figures such as Luther and Calvin, who would profess the same words Hus did, along with very similar viewpoints, more than a century later.[5]

In this book we have looked at several modern people for examples, never perfect of course, of the prophetic tradition's sensibilities. One feature all these moderns have in common is that, like Hus, they ran afoul of people in powerful positions. The critiques

3. Spinka, *John Hus: A Biography*, 133.

4. For more details on this treachery, see Spinka, *John Hus and the Czech Reform*, 53.

5. Ibid., 3.

these modern voices and Hus raised were rarely appreciated by people who were benefiting from the system that was being called into question. This pattern of shared experience is by no means accidental. In fact, it seems to be part and parcel of the role of prophetic spokesperson. In this chapter we look again at the biblical prophets with an eye toward the maltreatment they suffered, ranging from mild persecution to imprisonment and even death. After examining the biblical picture, we will turn again to the modern voices we have encountered in this book, illustrating the ways in which these courageous people have experienced similar treatment along the same spectrum—persecution, imprisonment, and, like Jan Hus, even death.

The legacy of prophetic abuse has deep roots in the ancient traditions. Already in the Old Testament there are allusions to the persistent rejection of the prophets and their message. In the long prayer in the book of Nehemiah that summarizes Israel's history, the people say, "[Our forefathers] were disobedient and rebelled against you [God]. They put your law behind their backs. They killed your prophets who had admonished them in order to turn them back to you" (Neh 9:26). A similar sentiment is found in the speech given by Stephen just before he was killed, when he reminded his Jewish audience that their forefathers had persecuted the prophets of old (Acts 7:52). Jesus himself invoked this tradition as a way to prepare his own disciples for the opposition they would meet (Matt 5:12).

Before turning to acts of outright persecution, it is worth recalling that the prophetic office was not infrequently associated with insanity. Hosea quotes one of the prevailing opinions about God's spokesmen: "The prophet is a fool, the man of the spirit is mad" (Hos 9:7). Jeremiah recounts a message that was sent to the priest Zephaniah son of Maaseiah, ordering him to take charge in the Temple of Yahweh "over every madman who prophesies, to put him in the stocks and collar" (Jer 29:26). These examples indicate that some in Israel assumed that those who prophesied were mentally unbalanced. This assumption extended to associates of the prophets as well; one of Jehu's men refers to Elisha's servant as a madman (2 Kgs 9:11).

Incidents of prophetic persecution in the Old Testament vary in intensity, ranging from verbal accusations of disloyalty or insanity to imprisonment, bodily harm, and even death. Elijah fled from Ahab and Jezebel because they were trying to kill the prophets of Yahweh (1 Kgs 18). In order to protect the true prophets that remained, a court official named Obadiah, a secret supporter of Elijah, had hidden them in caves and brought them provisions (1 Kgs 18:13). When Elijah met Ahab during this royal oppression, the king referred to him as a "troubler of Israel" (1 Kgs 18:17), and following the contest on Mount Carmel where Yahweh sent fire from heaven to demonstrate his power to the people, Elijah was on the run again in fear for his life. When he was fleeing from the royal persecution, Elijah complained to God that the Israelites had "killed your prophets with the sword" (1 Kgs 19:10, 14). No specific account of these deaths survives outside of these two comments from Elijah.

We noted in chapter 2 the story of Micaiah son of Imlah and his confrontation with Ahab that led to Micaiah speaking the prophetic word that Ahab would die at Ramoth Gilead. After this interchange at the royal court, Micaiah was hauled away to prison for speaking the truth. Also in chapter 2 we recounted the episode when the prophet Amos faced charges of sedition during his ministry to the Northern Kingdom (Amos 7:10–17). The priest Amaziah confronted him and accused him of undermining the king, Jeroboam II, and violating the sanctity of the royal sanctuary and a temple of the kingdom. Amos certainly trod upon the northern traditions of state-sponsored cult sites. What happened to Amos afterward is not recorded, but at the very least the priest Amaziah sought to expel Amos from the region, and the overall tenor of the story suggests that there were a number of people in the north who would have preferred to see Amos depart as well.

The prophet Jeremiah faced execution after he encouraged the people of Jerusalem to surrender to the Babylonians (Jer 38). Officials of King Zedekiah advised the king to kill Jeremiah for his words. The king handed Jeremiah over to them and they put the prophet in an empty water cistern. Their intent was to let him starve to death, according to the report given to the king by Jeremiah's rescuer, Eved-Melek (Jer 38:9–10). There was a similar incident where Jeremiah faced death after he had preached the so-called Temple Sermon (Jer 26). When the people heard his words of warning about the assumed unassailability of the Jerusalem temple, they quickly turned violent—indeed, the priests, prophets, and the people all wanted to seize Jeremiah in order to kill him (Jer 26:7). Although Jeremiah lived through this attempt on his life, another true prophet named Uriah was less fortunate. Like Jeremiah, Uriah also predicted doom for Jerusalem. Unlike Jeremiah, however, a king succeeded in killing him. Uriah fled to Egypt upon discovering that King Jehoiakim wanted him dead, but he was kidnapped by agents of the king and brought back to Israel to face execution (Jer 26:23).

One prophet escaped imprisonment precisely because he was a prophet. An unnamed prophet from Judah journeyed to Bethel to pronounce judgment on the altar that King Jeroboam I had erected there (1 Kgs 13). When the king heard the prophet's condemnation, he ordered his men to seize the man. But as soon as the king gave the order, his arm immediately withered, at which point the king begged the prophet to intercede for him.

The story of a prophet named Zechariah is told by the Chronicler (2 Chr 24:17–22). (This Zechariah is not the prophet for whom the book of Zechariah is named, who was active in the postexilic period.) During the reign of King Joash, Zechariah spoke against the sinful practices of the king. As a result, Joash's men had him killed.

It is easy to see why the tradition of ill treatment of the ancient prophets had achieved legendary status by the time of Jesus and Stephen. Christians will no doubt note that John the Baptist, Jesus, and even Stephen himself became part of this tradition in the New Testament. All three spoke the truth and stood for what is right. All three were tragically executed for their courage.

We now turn to each of the modern examples used in this book to illustrate the ways in which they, like the prophets of old, ran afoul of the powers that be and found themselves in some sort of trouble.

MYLES HORTON

We begin with Myles Horton. During the 1950s, the easiest way to demonize a US citizen was to suggest that they were communist. This accusation was directed at a number of the modern examples of the prophetic tradition in this book. At that moment in US history such a charge would not just ostracize someone; it could provoke a federal investigation. Of the modern figures discussed here, perhaps the one most affected by the charge of communism was Horton. Segregationists hated Highlander's commitment to integration, and industry management hated it because of the school's commitment to helping organize working people. Yet in the wake of the 1954 *Brown v. Board of Education* decision, which overturned the notion of "separate but equal" in public schools, segregationists knew that Highlander could not be charged with violating Jim Crow laws. Those in industrial circles knew that labor laws had long protected—at least in the abstract—working peoples' right to organize. So these two groups of people who were irritated by Highlander needed to formulate a complaint that the federal government would recognize and pursue. The charge of communism provided the necessary catalyst for federal censure.

Following World War II and the emergence of the Soviet Union as a world power, fear of communism's spread was pervasive in the US. The leading crusader against communist influence during this period was Wisconsin senator Joseph R. McCarthy, who fanned the anxiety over communism into hysteria. During the McCarthy hearings, designed to ferret out any communist sympathizers, a professional informer named Paul Crouch claimed that in Monteagle, Tennessee, members of the Communist Party were employed at the Highlander School run by Myles Horton and James Dombrowski. Horton responded to these accusations by claiming that people were confusing Highlander's "democratic policy," which called for equal treatment for all people regardless of race, with communism.[6]

It is no surprise that the number of state and federal investigations into Highlander increased after the *Brown v. Board of Education* decision. In 1954 a Senate internal security subcommittee made the institution part of an official probe. Three years later, the IRS temporarily revoked Highlander's tax-exempt status. Leaders in the South had attributed some of the responsibility for the organization of the civil rights movement to Highlander simply by virtue of the fact that some of the movement's leaders had attended workshops at the school. Such ties spelled guilt by association in the eyes of Horton's enemies, and by 1957 state governments had begun to take action. In that year the Georgia Commission on Education mounted a propaganda campaign against Highlander. In 1958 the Arkansas attorney general joined the hunt for subversive activity at the school.[7] The decade ended with the state of Tennessee raiding the school under the direction of a state district attorney and putting Horton and Highlander on trial twice. These actions climaxed with the repeal of Highlander's state charter and the confiscation of the school's property in 1962.

Some of the harassment Horton faced was on a more personal level. He was often denounced by church leaders in the regions where he traveled to assist with striking workers. As I noted in chapter 6, the most famous churchman to denounce Horton was Billy Sunday, who preached against him in the 1930s because of his work with striking miners and woodcutters in East Tennessee. Sunday was instrumental in stirring up popular mistrust of Horton and Highlander and prevented the school from receiving a $7,000 federal grant that had been allocated for the school in 1935.[8]

On other occasions, the resistance leveled at Horton was more sinister and sometimes outright dangerous. Horton tells

6. Glen, *Highlander*, 209.

7. All of these dates come from Glen, *Highlander*, 207.

8. Adams, *Unearthing Seeds of Fire*, 38–9.

of one instance in Lumberton, North Carolina, a small Southern town where he had been invited by workers to help with a strike. Virtually everyone in the town except the workers he was helping wanted him to leave. Even the churches of the town held prayer services asking God to force Horton's departure. One afternoon, looking out of a window in the hotel where he was staying, he noticed that there was hardly anyone on the streets. It seemed to him as if the town had abruptly shut down in the middle of the day. The sheriff's office appeared to have been abandoned, along with the courthouse. When a car with four men inside pulled up beside his hotel, Horton was certain they had come for him. He shouted down to them from his hotel window, claiming that he knew what they were planning. Horton took out a gun that a Holiness Pentecostal preacher had given to him earlier and displayed it to the four men in the car. He told them that he had spent his whole life helping people organize to make decisions, and since this might be his last chance to do so, he wanted to help them organize too. The men laughed and dismissed Horton's offer. Horton told them that they should probably reconsider, because they needed to decide which one of them was going to die that afternoon. Horton admitted that they outnumbered him. But since he was pretty sure that he could get at least one shot off from his pistol before they overpowered him, the group needed to choose a victim. Horton continued to banter with his would-be assailants, reminding them that their families would probably miss them if they died in this fight and thus individualizing them just as he did when he helped workers to organize. Eventually the car pulled away and Horton breathed a sigh of relief, wondering whether he had almost met his end that day. Horton told interviewers later that this was the best organizing speech he had ever given.[9] These accounts are just a sampling of the various forms of persecution that Horton and

---

9. Horton, interview with Bill Moyers. The story also appears in Adams, *Unearthing Seeds of Fire*, 64–66. I have blended details derived from both in this account.

the Highlander Folk School endured from individuals and from government organizations.[10]

CÉSAR CHÁVEZ

Like Myles Horton, César Chávez was accused of being a communist because of his efforts in support of working people, especially the working poor. Earlier we noted the work Chávez did in organizing people employed on grape farms in California. When the efforts to unmask the oppressive labor practices of the grape growers grew violent in December 1965, Chávez called for a boycott of grapes. Early the next year the growers used their crop-dusting planes to spray picket lines of striking workers with dangerous pesticides.[11] The growers harassed, beat, and shot striking farmworkers—often with tacit assistance from local law enforcement.[12] Chávez and his striking workers also came under the censure of the California state government. Governor Ronald Reagan labeled the boycott "immoral" and referred to the strikers as "barbarians."[13]

Chávez also drew the hostility of the Catholic Church in California because of his advocacy of migrant farm laborers at large grape orchards. Daniel Lyons and Cletus Healy, two Jesuit priests who served under the local bishop in Fresno, attacked Chávez in a conservative Catholic newspaper called *Twin Circle*. These two priests served on a committee formed by the bishop to address the concerns Chávez and the workers raised. Lyons insisted that Chávez was a fraud, and Healy claimed that Chávez had little support among most of the workers.[14]

The growers in the region were, like many of the workers, devout Catholics. Yet many of them were of Irish, Italian, or Slavic

10. The examples could be easily multiplied and readers who would like to know more should consult the very fine work by Glen, *Highlander*, especially 207–50.

11. O'Brien, "La Causa," 156.

12. Prouty, *César Chávez*, 29.

13. Ibid., 29–30.

14. Ibid., 33.

descent and did not readily connect with the Spanish-speaking Catholics who worked on their farms. It was often said that the Catholic Church in the grape-growing region was financed by the growers, but the pews were filled with the workers and their families. Because of this reality, the church authorities tried to tread lightly so as to avoid involvement in the rising conflict between the growers and the laborers. Chávez pressed the church to support the workers, in spite of threats by the wealthy growers to withdraw financial support from the church. Resisting pressure to accept the status quo, Chávez risked trouble with the church leaders in his efforts to convince them that it was the mission of the church to care for the struggling workers. Chastised by some of the more conservative priests and bishops, Chávez was unmoved, and eventually his point of view was embraced by the church.

DOROTHY DAY

Dorothy Day encountered a number of threats during her lifetime as well. Much of the harassment she faced originated within the Catholic hierarchy. Like Horton and Chávez, Day was an easy target for the charge of communism throughout her life. She had, after all, worked for *The Call*, an avidly socialist newspaper, when she was a teenager, and many of her close friends were anarchists, socialists, or communists. We noted in chapter 1 that she was imprisoned with the suffragettes when they marched on Washington in 1917. On more than one occasion she ran afoul of Catholic power structures on the issue of fair treatment of workers, as we noted in chapter 6. Day's newspaper, *The Catholic Worker*, raised the hackles of many a conservative Catholic in the 1940s and 50s, especially during the "red scare" fueled by Senator McCarthy's hearings. In the early years of her work many believed that the terms "Catholic" and "worker" simply did not go together. Day was shunned by many Catholics in the 1930s during the Spanish Civil War, since she refused to support Franco's republicans, who were backed by the Catholic Church and Nazi Germany. Her refusal to take a side at all in this conflict meant that she was ostracized by both sides. Day's commitment to pacifism during the 1930s and 40s was fully out of step with most Americans, especially after the Japanese bombed Pearl Harbor on December 7, 1941. Dorothy Day demonstrated a profound moral courage by maintaining her convictions despite these numerous social pressures.

During the Cold War, Day refused to participate in the mandatory drills to prepare for nuclear attack held in New York City. When the sirens sounded on June 15, 1955, Day was among a small group of protesters sitting in front of City Hall. "In the name of Jesus, who is God, who is Love, we will not obey this order to pretend, to evacuate, to hide. We will not be drilled into fear. We do not have faith in God if we depend upon the Atom Bomb," a *Catholic Worker* leaflet explained. Although the dissidents were merely reprimanded in 1955, Day and others were sent to jail for five days after the 1956 drill. When she was arrested again in the following year, the judge jailed her for thirty days. In 1958, a different judge suspended the sentence. In 1959, Day was back in prison, but only for five days. Then came 1960, when the handful of demonstrators expected to gather at City Hall Park turned out to number five hundred. The police arrested only a few people, and Day was conspicuously not among those singled out for booking. In 1961 the crowd of protestors swelled to two thousand. This time forty were arrested, but again Day was exempt. Her persistence paid off, however, because 1961 proved to be the last year of dress rehearsals for nuclear war in New York City.[15]

Sometimes Day was threatened with bodily harm for reasons that had nothing to do with ideology. She told a story of a drunken sailor who came to one of her houses of hospitality one evening. The man was very angry, and she thought he might be a bit deranged since he growled like a dog at the people near him. The man's rage grew to the point where he threatened to kill everyone there. Although Dorothy was very frightened herself, she approached the sailor calmly and talked to him gently, offering him some soup. The tense moment passed when he realized that

15. The details of this story are recounted in Piehl, "*Catholic Worker* in the Early Cold War Era," 86–88.

Dorothy was no threat to him. Eventually he ate the soup, and a few days later he returned with vegetables that he wanted to contribute to the kitchen. Dorothy happily reported that this man soon became one of their regulars.[16]

CORNEL WEST

Cornel West is the youngest of the modern voices considered here. His experiences of persecution have not been as dramatic as being hauled before Congress or repeatedly imprisoned. West has received his share of death threats, however, from a number of hate groups.[17] He was arrested in 2011 for publically demonstrating against New York City's "stop and frisk" program. West has also written from a personal, experiential perspective about the kinds of discrimination many African Americans face each day.[18]

WILL CAMPBELL

Will Campbell received death threats throughout his career too. On one occasion his father begged him to stay out of Mississippi because there was a KKK bounty on his head.[19] More often, however, he experienced less perilous forms of harassment. Campbell began his first job at a college when he was hired as the campus minister at the University of Mississippi, a state-funded position. After inviting a local minister who was black to visit the campus and play table tennis in the student center, Campbell was called in by the dean to explain himself. As Campbell tells it, he informed the dean that "it was all in keeping with the old Southern pattern. We had separate but equal paddles, we had a net drawn between

---

16. This story was recounted by Day to Robert Coles. See Coles, *Dorothy Day*, 122–25.

17. West, interview with Brian Lamb.

18. See West, *Race Matters*, especially xiv–xvi.

19. Letcher, *God's Will*.

us, and . . . well, the dean did not think it was very funny."[20] After this incident, someone put feces in the punch bowl at a college ministry function.

Earlier that year Campbell had helped to defend a local community health clinic that served blacks and whites. The clinic was being picketed by local Citizens' Councils, a white-supremacist organization committed to propping up Jim Crow segregation laws. Wealthy donors to the school demanded that the president fire Campbell for lending support to the integrated clinic. And so Campbell was called into the president's office. Around the same time, Campbell invited an Episcopalian priest to speak on the campus. The priest had openly voiced his support for the civil rights movement on a nationally televised game show, and as a result he had become a controversial figure in the South. The president of Ole Miss demanded that Campbell rescind his invitation to the priest, but he refused. These events culminated in Campbell's eventual resignation from the University of Mississippi.

MARTIN L. KING JR.

The most tragic modern figure considered in this book is, of course, Martin Luther King Jr. He was arrested many times and spent time in jail for civil disobedience and standing for what was right. Trouble began for King during the Montgomery Bus Boycott, which lasted just over a year (December 1, 1955–December 20, 1956). King was arrested for the first time in January 1956 on a trumped-up charge of speeding when he was serving as a driver in the car pool organized to help participants in the boycott get to work and return home. After his release, King's home telephone began ringing with thirty or forty death threats per day. On January 30, only two months into the bus boycott, King's house was firebombed while King's wife, Coretta Scott King, and their baby were inside.[21] Remarkably no one was physically harmed.

20. Campbell relates this story in Letcher, *God's Will.*

21. These dates and other information are from Carson, *Autobiography of Martin Luther King,* 65-75.

King was arrested again one month later on charges of violating an old state law outlawing boycotts. On March 22, 1956, King was convicted of this charge and had to pay a $500 fine. Even after the Supreme Court declared the Montgomery bus segregation unconstitutional and decreed that all persons were free to sit anywhere on the buses, the violence continued. On January 28, 1957, King's house in Montgomery was targeted once again, but on this occasion the twelve sticks of dynamite planted on the porch failed to explode. King was also the victim of an attack by a deranged woman in Harlem while he was signing autographs in a store there on September 20, 1958. The knife she used narrowly missed his aorta and so King escaped death by a thin margin that day.

King was arrested a number of other times for participating in organized sit-ins in Atlanta on October 19, 1960, and in Albany, Georgia, on December 15, 1961. Convicted of leading the protest in Albany, King was sentenced to forty-five days in jail (but his fine was paid by an anonymous donor). He was also harassed with petty charges like falsifying income tax returns in February 1960 (a charge of which he was later acquitted) and driving in Georgia with an Alabama driver's license in October 1960. For this offense King was shackled like a vicious criminal and bused to the state prison in Reidsville, 220 miles away. A phone call from US Attorney General Robert Kennedy expedited King's release on that particular occasion.

Perhaps his most famous incarceration took place in the Birmingham city jail in April, 1963. King had come to Birmingham to organize direct actions including sit-ins, boycotts of downtown stores, and marches. On Good Friday, April 12, King and Ralph Abernathy defied a court order that they cease all demonstrations. Both men were arrested along with other participants in the march and King was put in solitary confinement. After more phone calls on his behalf from President John F. Kennedy and his brother Robert, the attorney general, King's incarceration conditions improved. He was permitted to receive the newspaper, where he read an open letter from eight local clergymen calling for him to cease the direct action in Birmingham. His response to them, dated April 16, became the famous "Letter from Birmingham City Jail." He and Abernathy were released three days later on April 19.

Yet even after their release the violence continued. On May 11, 1963, the Gaston Hotel where King was residing was bombed, as was the home of King's brother, A. D. King. Arrests and imprisonment continued as well. The following year, on June 11, King was arrested in St. Augustine, Florida, for demonstrating for civil rights there, and on February 1, 1965, King was arrested in Selma, Alabama, for demonstrating in support of voting rights.

Of all the persecution that Martin Luther King Jr. experienced—harassment, imprisonment, and attempts on his life—what makes King's story the most tragic is his assassination in Memphis by a sniper on April 4, 1968. He was just thirty-nine years old.

CONCLUSION

None of the courageous people we have examined in this chapter sought out trouble for its own sake. Trouble came to them because they had the courage and strength to stand up and speak the truth. The same is true of the biblical prophets as well: they did not deliberately seek out conflict, but their messages frequently spurred their opponents to act against them. Nevertheless, the testimony of these modern-day examples is a reminder that conflict is virtually inevitable for those who have the courage to question the status quo. It is no coincidence that all of these people experienced the kind of resistance that many of the biblical prophets encountered. Such a situation is part and parcel of walking in the prophetic tradition.

Conclusion

Of the modern voices we have examined in this book, three of them have gone on to garner great respect in many circles today. Although despised by many in her lifetime, Dorothy Day is now being considered for sainthood. The process began in 2000 when the Vatican initiated the canonization process for Day, naming her a "Servant of God." In a 2012 meeting of US bishops, Cardinal Timothy Dolan of New York called Dorothy Day "a saint for our time," describing her as "a living, breathing, colorful, lovable, embracing, warm woman who exemplifies what's best in Catholic life" and shows the church's commitment to both the dignity of human life and social justice.

Likewise, Martin L. King Jr. has become the most recognized representative of the American civil rights movement. A federal holiday and a monument in Washington, DC, attest to the broad recognition in the US of the value of King's work. His likeness has even been placed in one of the ten niches over the main entrance of London's Westminster Abbey, along with those of other martyred heroes.

Additionally, César Chávez is now widely recognized for his work on behalf of farm laborers and immigrant communities. In 1994 Chávez was posthumously awarded the Presidential Medal of Freedom by President Bill Clinton. On March 31, a number of US states celebrate César Chávez Day as a state holiday on which all are called to community service.

The passage of time has attenuated the hatred that many harbored against these three people when they were alive. Like the biblical prophets of old, their message, once an object of derision in their own day, achieved a new level of widespread appreciation among later generations. Greater acceptance and appreciation for the work of Day, King, and Chavez today illustrates the discerning community's ability to bend in the direction of justice—doing the right thing. Such a transition should give everyone pause about people who are demonized in the present for their advocacy of controversial issues. They too might be part of the prophetic tradition in our day—derided now, but destined to be upheld as heroes in years to come. The process of discernment, which is deeply rooted in the biblical prophetic stance, can provide clarity in the here and now that will be confirmed with the passage of time.

It is my sincere hope that this book can be a small contribution to the effort to equip us all with a deeper appreciation for God's work in the world in the past and present. By juxtaposing the ancient prophetic message with the words and deeds of modern people, I hope to have achieved two things, namely, to provide a helpful lens to understand how the biblical prophets might have been viewed in their day, while at the same time demonstrating how we can look to modern people, committed to similar ideals, as models for us today.

The quest to apply the message of the biblical prophets has been a perennial struggle for the people of God. The interpretation of these ancient voices by the New Testament writers and by the early church fathers established trajectories that highlighted predictive elements and connections with the ministry of Jesus. Amidst the polemics between Christian and Jewish communities, Christian interpreters often appropriated the prophetic texts that could most easily be aligned with some aspect of Jesus' ministry and, as a result, often ignored the prophetic critiques of power and excess. For different reasons, the Constantinian Shift also encouraged a selective use of the prophetic corpus. Both the Old and New Testaments were forced to speak the language of empire, and the biblical critique of the abuse of power was effectively silenced so as not to offend the powers of the day. The prophetic voice was virtually domesticated within most Christian communities. When these sociological trends—the separation of Christians from Jews and the recognition of Christianity by the state—converged during the fourth century CE, the prophetic witness against power was mostly silenced, shackled by the concerns for the safety and security of nascent Christendom.

Yet the domestication of the prophets' voices was never absolute, and over the last two millennia we can find tokens of the undomesticated prophetic word among certain individuals. At times their voices were faint and the flame of their commitment was perhaps dim. Even today the number of people committed to hearing the prophetic voice in all its unbridled splendor is not as great as some might think. The challenge for all is to become aware of how the prophetic tradition is in danger of being domesticated again in our day, and of how its voice can be silenced or transmuted to blunt its purpose. To keep the prophetic light shining, attending to the biblical accounts of the prophets and to the biographies of modern people who embraced the struggle for justice is a good start—a good start on a journey that has us walking in the prophetic tradition.

Bibliography

Adams, Frank, with Myles Horton, *Unearthing Seeds of Fire: The Idea of Highlander*. Winston-Salem, NC: Blair, 1975.

Appleby, Joyce. "The Intellectual Underpinnings of American Democracy." *Daedalus* 136 (2007) 14–23.

Bembry, Jason. "Cornel West, Biblical Transparency, and American Historical Amnesia." *Theology Today* 68 (2011) 123–33.

———. "The Levite's Concubine (Judg 19:2) and the Tradition of Sexual Slander in the Hebrew Bible: How the Nature of Her Departure Illustrates a Tradition's Tendency." *Vetus Testamentum*, forthcoming.

Bender, Steven W. *One Night in America: Robert Kennedy, César Chávez, and the Dream of Dignity*. New York: Routledge, 2015.

———. *Tierra y Libertad: Land, Liberty and Latino Housing*. New York: New York University Press, 2010.

Birch, Bruce C. *Let Justice Roll Down: The Old Testament, Ethics, and Christian Life*. Louisville: Westminster John Knox, 1991.

Blenkinsopp, Joseph. *A History of Prophecy in Israel*. Louisville: Westminster John Knox, 1996.

Brettler, Marc. "The Book of Judges: Literature as Politics." *Journal of Biblical Literature* 108 (1989) 395–418.

Campbell, Will D. *Brother to a Dragonfly*. New York: Continuum, 2000.

———. "Can There Be a Crusade for Christ?" In *Writings on Reconciliation and Resistance*, edited by Richard C. Goode, 128–33. Eugene, OR: Cascade Books, 2010.

———. "Exchange of Letters with Chaplain Amos L. Wilson, Tennessee State Prison." In *Writings on Reconciliation and Resistance*, edited by Richard C. Goode, 26–30. Eugene, OR: Cascade Books, 2010.

Campbell, Will D., and James Y. Holloway. "An Open Letter to Dr. Billy Graham." *Katallagete* (Winter 1971) 1–4. Reprinted in *Writings on Reconciliation and Resistance*, edited by Richard C. Goode, 124–27. Eugene, OR: Cascade Books, 2010.

Carson, Clayborne, ed., *The Autobiography of Martin Luther King, Jr.* New York: Warner, 1998.

Chávez, César. *The Gospel of César Chávez: My Faith in Action.* Edited by Mario T. García. Lanham, MD: Sheed & Ward, 2007.

Coles, Robert. *Dorothy Day: A Radical Devotion.* Reading, MA: Addison-Wesley, 1987.

Day, Dorothy. *The Long Loneliness: The Autobiography of Dorothy Day.* San Francisco: Harper & Row, 1952.

———. "Love Is the Measure." *The Catholic Worker*, June 1946, 2.

Finkelstein, Israel, Shlomo Bunimovitz, and Zvi Lederman. *Shiloh: The Archaeology of a Biblical Site.* Tel Aviv Monograph Series 10. Tel Aviv: Tel Aviv University, 1993.

Fleming, Daniel E. "Ur: After the Gods Abandoned Us." *Classical World* 97/1 (2003) 5–18.

Glen, John M. *Highlander: No Ordinary School.* Knoxville: University of Tennessee Press, 1996.

Hatch, Nathan O. *The Democratization of American Christianity.* New Haven: Yale University Press, 1989.

Heschel, Abraham J. *The Prophets.* New York: Harper, 1962.

Horton, Myles. Interview with Bill Moyers, "The Adventures of a Radical Hillbilly: Part 1." *Bill Moyers' Journal.* WNET Productions. Aired on PBS, June 5, 1981.

Kaiser, Otto. *Isaiah 1–12.* 2nd ed. Translated by John Bowden. Old Testament Library. Philadelphia: Westminster, 1983.

King, Martin Luther Jr. "The American Dream." In *A Testament of Hope: The Essential Writings and Speeches of Martin Luther King, Jr.*, edited by James Melvin Washington, 208–16. New York: HarperOne, 1986.

———. "Behind the Selma March." In *A Testament of Hope: The Essential Writings and Speeches of Martin Luther King, Jr.*, edited by James Melvin Washington, 126–31. New York: HarperOne, 1986.

———. "I See the Promised Land." In *A Testament of Hope: The Essential Writings and Speeches of Martin Luther King, Jr.*, edited by James Melvin Washington, 279–86. New York: HarperOne, 1986.

———. "Letter from Birmingham City Jail." In *A Testament of Hope: The Essential Writings and Speeches of Martin Luther King, Jr.*, edited by James Melvin Washington, 289–302. New York: HarperOne, 1986.

———. "The Most Durable Power." In *A Testament of Hope: The Essential Writings and Speeches of Martin Luther King, Jr.*, edited by James Melvin Washington, 10–11. New York: HarperOne, 1986.

———. "Nonviolence and Racial Justice." In *A Testament of Hope: The Essential Writings and Speeches of Martin Luther King, Jr.*, edited by James Melvin Washington, 5–9. New York: HarperOne, 1986.

———. "Our Struggle." In *A Testament of Hope: The Essential Writings and Speeches of Martin Luther King, Jr.*, edited by James Melvin Washington, 75–81. New York: HarperOne, 1986.

————. "*Playboy* Interview: Martin Luther King, Jr." In *A Testament of Hope: The Essential Writings and Speeches of Martin Luther King, Jr.*, edited by James Melvin Washington, 340–77. New York: HarperOne, 1986.

————. "The Power of Nonviolence." In *A Testament of Hope: The Essential Writings and Speeches of Martin Luther King, Jr.*, edited by James Melvin Washington, 12–15. New York: HarperOne, 1986.

Kugel, James L. "Topics in the History of the Spirituality of the Psalms." In *Jewish Spirituality: From the Bible through the Middle Ages*, edited by Arthur Green, 113–44. New York: Crossroad, 1987.

Letcher, Michael. *God's Will*. Documentary film directed by Michael Letcher. Tuscaloosa: University of Alabama Center for Public Television, 2000.

Levenson, Jon D. "The Temple and the World." *Journal of Religion* 64 (1984) 275–98.

Lundbom, Jack R. *Jeremiah 1–20*. Anchor Bible 21A. New York: Doubleday, 1999.

Lützow, Franz Heinrich. *The Life and Times of Master John Hus*. New York: E. P. Dutton, 1978.

MacIntosh, A. A. *Hosea*. International Critical Commentary. Edinburgh: T. & T. Clark, 1997.

Mays, James L. *Amos*. Old Testament Library. Philadelphia: Westminster, 1969.

Miller, Robert J. *Helping Jesus Fulfill Prophecy*. Eugene, OR: Cascade Books, 2014.

Miranda, José Porfirio. *Marx and the Bible: A Critique of the Philosophy of Oppression*. Translated by John Eagleson. 1974. Reprint, Eugene, OR: Wipf & Stock, 2004.

Nelson, Richard D. *Deuteronomy*. Old Testament Library. Louisville: Westminster John Knox, 2002.

Nissinen, Martti, ed. *Prophecy in Its Ancient Near Eastern Context*. SBL Symposium Series 13. Atlanta: SBL, 2000.

O'Brien, Kevin J. "'La Causa' and Environmental Justice: César Chávez as a Resource for Christian Ecological Ethics." *Journal of the Society of Christian Ethics* 32 (2012) 151–68.

Paul, Shalom. *Amos*. Hermeneia. Minneapolis: Fortress, 1991.

Piehl, Mel. "The *Catholic Worker* and Peace in the Early Cold War Era." In *American Catholic Pacifism: The Influence of Dorothy Day and the Catholic Worker Movement*, edited by Anne Klejment and Nancy L. Roberts, 77–90. Westport, CT: Praeger, 1996.

Pritchard, James B., ed. *Ancient Near Eastern Texts Relating to the Old Testament*. 3rd ed. with supplement. Princeton: Princeton University Press, 1969.

Prouty, Marco G. *César Chávez, the Catholic Bishops, and the Farmworkers' Struggle for Social Justice*. Tucson: University of Arizona Press, 2006.

Reimer, A. James. *Christians and War*. Minneapolis: Fortress, 2010.

Sandel, Michael J. *Liberalism and the Limits of Justice*. 2nd ed. Cambridge: Cambridge University Press, 1998.

Sawyer, John F. A. *The Fifth Gospel: Isaiah in the History of Christianity.* Cambridge: Cambridge University Press, 1996.

Schley, Donald G. *Shiloh: A Biblical City in Tradition and History.* Sheffield: Sheffield Academic, 1989.

Schneider, Stephen A. *You Can't Padlock an Idea: Rhetorical Education at the Highlander Folk School, 1932–1961.* Studies in Rhetoric/Communication. Columbia: University of South Carolina Press, 2014.

Skarsaune, Oskar. "The Development of Scriptural Interpretation in the Second and Third Centuries—except Clement and Origen." In *Hebrew Bible / Old Testament: The History of Its Interpretation,* vol. 1, edited by Magne Sæbø, 373–442. Göttingen: Vandenhoeck & Ruprecht, 1996.

Spinka, Matthew. *John Hus: A Biography.* Princeton: Princeton University Press, 1968.

———. *John Hus and the Czech Reform.* Hamden, CT: Archon, 1966.

Tocqueville, Alexis de. *Democracy in America.* New York: Century, 1898.

West, Cornel. *Democracy Matters.* New York: Penguin, 2004.

———. Interview with Brian Lamb on *Booknotes.* C-SPAN cable network. February 22, 2000.

———. Interview with Christopher Lydon on *The Connection.* WBUR-FM. December 20, 1999.

———. "Introduction: To Be Human, Modern, and American." In *The Cornel West Reader,* xvi–xviii. New York: Basic Civitas, 1999.

———. *Prophesy Deliverance.* Louisville: Westminster John Knox, 2002.

———. *Prophetic Fragments: Illuminations of the Crisis of American Religion and Culture.* Grand Rapids: Eerdmans, 1988.

———. *Prophetic Reflections: Notes on Race and Power in America.* Monroe, ME: Common Courage, 1993.

———. *Prophetic Thought in Postmodern Times.* Monroe, ME: Common Courage, 1993.

———. *Race Matters.* New York: Vintage, 1993.

Wolff, Hans W. *Hosea.* Translated by Gary Stansell. Hermeneia. Philadelphia: Fortress, 1974.

Zinn, Howard. *A People's History of the United States.* New York: HarperCollins, 2003.

Scripture Index

CPSIA information can be obtained
at www.ICGtesting.com
Printed in the USA
LVHW010106280420
654624LV00005B/1626